New York City with Kids

Open Road *is* Travel!

OPEN ROAD TRAVEL GUIDES:
THE ONLY WAY TO SEE PLANET EARTH

Whether you're going abroad or planning a trip in the United States, take Open Road along on your journey. Our books have been praised by **Travel & Leisure, The Los Angeles Times, Newsday, Booklist, US News & World Report, Endless Vacation, American Bookseller, Coast to Coast,** and many other magazines and newspapers!

Don't just see the world – experience it with Open Road!

About the Author

Laurie Bain Wilson is a travel writer whose specialty is family travel. Her other books include *The Unofficial Guide to New England and New York with Kids*. She lives in Sea Cliff, New York, with her son Alex.

Open Road *is* Travel!

Open Road Publishing has guide books to exciting, fun destinations on four continents. As veteran travelers, our goal is to bring you the best travel guides available anywhere!

No small task, but here's what we offer:

• All Open Road travel guides are written by authors with a distinct, opinionated point of view – not some sterile committee or team of writers. Our authors are experts in the areas covered and are polished writers.

• Our guides are geared to people who want to make their own travel choices. We'll show you how to discover the real destination – not just see some place from a tour bus window.

• We're strong on the basics, but we also provide terrific choices for those looking to get off the beaten path and experience the country or city – not just see it or pass through it.

• We give you the best, but we also tell you about the worst and what to avoid. Nobody should waste their time and money on their hard-earned vacation because of bad or inadequate travel advice.

• Our guides assume nothing. We tell you everything you need to know to have the trip of a lifetime – presented in a fun, literate, no-nonsense style.

• And, above all, we welcome your input, ideas, and suggestions to help us put out the best travel guides possible.

New York City with Kids

Open Road *is* Travel!

Laurie Bain Wilson

Open Road Publishing

Open Road Publishing

We offer travel guides to American and foreign locales. Our books tell it like it is, often with an opinionated edge, and our experienced authors always give you all the information you need to have the trip of a lifetime. Write for your free catalog of all our titles.

Open Road Publishing
P.O. Box 284, Cold Spring Harbor, NY 11724
E-mail: Jopenroad@aol.com

To Alexander, or AWIL, always keep your head high and your glove down.

Acknowledgments

A special thanks to Jackie Bain, my mother, who is from Boston but roots for the Yankees and always for me and Alex; to Donald Bain, my father and writing mentor; to Pam, Stu, Zach, Jake and Luke, let's meet in the City; to Rebecca Brubaker for always being there with love and food; to Colleen Brewer, you are my hero; to awesome seven-year-old Morgan Coutts; to Sea Cliff friends and families who helped with this book; to all of the 9/11 Cantor Fitzgerald families whose faces I will never forget; many thanks to editor and publisher Jonathan Stein for his unwavering support, as well as his enthusiasm for New York's family-friendly treasures; and finally, to New Yorkers, who are simply the best.

Contents

7. THE OUTER BOROUGHS   110

8. I'M HUNGRY!   122

9. WHICH ONE IS MY ROOM?   145

10. FIELD TRIPS   161

MAPS

New York City with Kids

১

1. INTRODUCTION

My son Alex was born in New York City, a town millions of children call home. These kids love to share their backyard (Central Park), their playgrounds, their restaurants, their favorite museums and their passion for New York. They make sure the Big Apple doesn't lose its youthful charm, despite being the most sophisticated and cosmopolitan of cities.

Yet, it's no secret that there was a plan to kill New York's soul, to rip out its heart and to destroy its reputation as the world's most sensational city. *Fuhgedaboudit!*

Dreams don't die in New York. Hope is around every corner and even the brattiest of New Yorkers stroll wide-and-starry-eyed at the city's wonders. And every morning brings the promise of a new discovery, a new treat for the senses.

September 11 personified New York, and New Yorkers—of every age— have become fiercely defensive of their City while also extremely generous in showing visitors a good time. Tourists, too, are protective of this great city that was so badly wounded and have come out in force; in 2003, the City welcomed more than 36 million tourists who have embraced the city in solidarity and in awe of the dignity of its people. According to a recent marketing survey, New York was ranked one of the top five places that parents wanted to vacation with their children. In fact, 16 percent of tourists to the City are families, accounting for 3.3 million people a year.

The City's spirit is as contagious as a deep belly laugh—you'll catch it and pass it along. Promise. Yes, you'll find some crab apples and worms in the Big Apple. But, when you pack up to return home, you'll agree that New York is one helluva town.

Chapter 2

OVERVIEW

As a travel editor and writer for my entire professional career, I have traveled to many wonderful distant spots around the world. When my son was born, I packed him along for journeys. We snorkeled in the Turks and Caicos, kayaked the still waters off Prince Edward Island, tracked down Mickey at Walt Disney World, fired up the barbecue on Cape Cod beaches and munched on the sweetest pineapple in Hawaii.

Yet, no matter how exciting or fabulous our trips are, when our plane flies over Manhattan to bring us home or our car crosses one of the bridges, I always get a rush. And, yet, I see magical Manhattan all the time. I can only imagine the thrill of experiencing it as a visitor.

From a distance, the City's skyline is a tease. Experience its neighborhoods and its people and New York flirts even more with incredible restaurants, enthralling attractions, mind-boggling museums and welcoming hotels. New York's reputation as a cultural Mecca is undeniable. From Broadway shows to Carnegie Hall concerts to Lincoln Center performances to the Metropolitan Museum of Art's exhibits, Manhattan is a canvas for the arts. Kudos, too, to the New York for recently being named the "Sporting Capital of the United States," home to the Knicks, Yankees, Mets, Rangers, U.S. Open Tennis and the New York City Marathon, to name just a few of the great sports teams and events. And at press time, New York City is still a contender to host the Olympics in 2012.

History Tidbits

From the get go, New York City's heart has always beat faster than in other places in the country—and the world. Downtown Manhattan was the

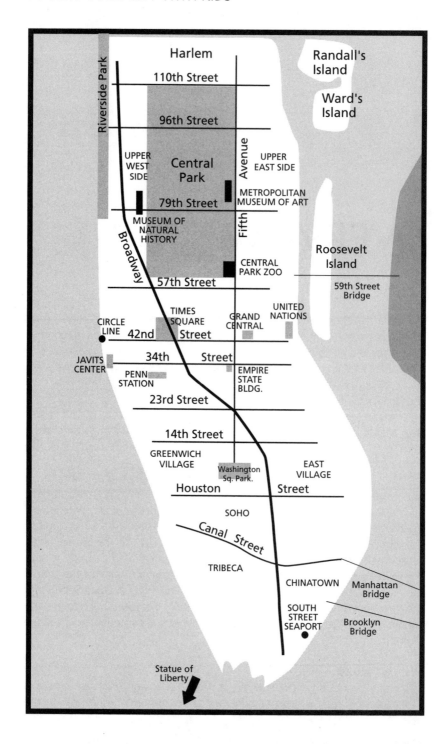

site of the nation's first Capital from 1789 to 1780 and was the U.S. Capital until 1797. Ellis Island embraced more than 12 million immigrants between 1892 and 1954. The Brooklyn Bridge was the world's longest suspension bridge (as well as the City's tallest structure) when it was built. The Cathedral Church of St. John the Divine is the world's largest gothic cathedral. Macy's is the world's largest store, covering 2.1 million square feet of space with more than 500,000 different items. The oldest municipal golf course, built in 1895, is in Van Cortlandt Park in the Bronx. And the New York Yankees have won more World Series championships (26) than any other Major League Baseball team.

Fun Facts: Giovanni da Verrazano is believed to have been the first European to explore the region and Henry Hudson is said to have visited, but it was the Dutch settlements that first began the city of New York. The town of New Amsterdam was established in 1624 on lower Manhattan when the island was bought from Native American inhabitants for $24 worth of trinkets. In 1664, the city's tallest structure was a two-story windmill. Under the Dutch settlement, Wall Street (yes, there really was a wall here) was the city limit.

• The English seized the colony (without firing a shot) in 1664 and renamed it New York City.

• The New York Stock Exchange (the world's largest exchange, trading $5.5 trillion annually) started in 1792 when 24 brokers met under a tree in downtown Manhattan. The New York Mercantile Exchange dates to the 1750's when it existed as the Butter and Cheese Exchange.

• The first ticker tape parade was in 1886 to celebrate the dedication of the Statue of Liberty. (There have been more than 200 ticker-tape parades in Lower Broadway's Canyon of Heroes.)

Travel Tips

A successful vacation in the City takes careful planning—but the plan should be flexible. That's the New York way. Have a plan—but remember things change here in a New York minute (that's the beauty of the City, really.) As parents, you know full well the importance of being able to go with the flow.

It's necessary also to build in extra time to get where you want to get. Traffic in New York can come to a crawl for any number of reasons—and often does. If you have theater tickets for an 8 o'clock show, build in lots of getting-there time. Word to the wise: If you're not sure, ask. New Yorkers are very friendly and love to give directions. They're fast talkers so pay attention, but they'll get you there the quickest way.

To ensure a successful family trip, keep the following pointers in mind:

• **Build in lots of down time.** That can mean hanging out at Central Park, at one of the City's playgrounds or at the hotel swimming pool. Wherever you choose to decompress, make sure you do it. New York is a vital town— you'll eventually feed off its energy (and so will your kids) and won't want to miss a beat. My son is always on the go, hates to be bored and I attribute this to living in the City. Your kids, too, will love all the excitement and want to keep going and going and going. But they'll burn out if you're not careful.

- **Make the trip as interactive as possible.** My son loves to have a map of wherever we are in our travels. You can pick up free maps at many places throughout the City, as well as subway maps, which kids also love. Also, encourage them to keep a journal of their days and nights in the Big Apple.

- **Part of the fun in New York is walking the streets**. My son and I often choose to walk rather than ride, no matter the distance. However, most kids who are visiting *love* riding the subways—to them it's an attraction, not a way of getting around.

- **Empower your children by getting them involved in planning the days' itineraries**. "Should we take the bus or subway?" "Do you think we should walk down East 45th Street or East 46th Street?"

- **Establish some kinds of routines**. For example, give each child $5 a day to spend; they can save it up to buy one thing at the end of the trip or buy something every day. Also, with younger children, don't skip meals— make sure they know there's breakfast, lunch and dinner every day, just like at home.

- **Try to avoid befuddled expectations**. Many kids are old enough and have traveled enough to have established reference points, but still have gaping voids in their mental pictures of their world. For example, when my son was young, he feared that the waffles he was served for breakfast at one of the authentic taverns at historic Colonial Williamsburg were also "old;" imagined that our car would tumble off one of Cape Breton's especially curvaceous roads in Nova Scotia; and expected to be able to pet the whales while on a whale watch excursion off Cape Cod. Anticipate and listen to what's going on in their minds.

- **Teens love headphones**. And they certainly can come in handy in keeping the peace. However, walking the streets of any city with music piped into your ears isn't the best idea in the world. New York is a town where you need to be alert (part of its allure, anyway, are the sounds of honking taxis, spirited conversations and street musicians).

- **Art museums can be a lot more enjoyable for kids of all ages if they have some background information** about what they are seeing. Most of the museums in the City have family guides or exhibit-related games and puzzles. Make sure to ask when you arrive at the museum.

- **A vacation for single parents and kids is an oxymoron**. New York is filled with tons of single parents and their kids so you won't feel alone. However, you most likely won't get any down time, either. Think about inviting a close friend or relative (or, more importantly, close friends of your children). This might be prohibitive because of the cost (hotel rooms in Manhattan tend to be small and there might not be enough room), but if you can, the trip might be more enjoyable. Unlike resort destinations, New York City is not the type of getaway where your child can hang out at a children's program while you sightsee or read a book on the beach. As a single parent, I find it helpful that the resort or hotel where we'll be staying has a reputable kid's program. Or, I scope out local programs for children where we're visiting. For example, while on the Cape last summer, I signed Alex up for a one-week baseball camp sponsored by the Cape Cod League Baseball organization held each morning from 9 am to noon. It was inexpensive and gave him a chance to play ball and to meet other children his age. It also bought me time to enjoy myself. A New York City vacation won't afford you the same kind of luxury. However, for older teens, you might consider investing in walkie-talkies, or a cell phone so you can give them some at least a little space—and for peace of mind in the event you get separated.

Chapter 3

PLANNING YOUR TRIP

Climate & Weather

New York City typically experiences Mother Nature's four seasons, although some years the city ducks the extreme winter and summer temps it is eligible for.

The winters can be frosty cold and snowy—or, mild and snow-free. If you find yourselves in a New York City snowstorm, rejoice! The pace in this hustle-bustle town almost comes to a halt and New Yorkers celebrate the event. You'll even see them cross-country skiing down Broadway.

Spring is a special time in the city but the weather can be finicky and rainy; some springs are downright cold.

Summers in New York are almost always humid and can sometimes be unbearably hot. The city is prone to heat waves and by day two or three of one of these spells the subways and streets can be insufferable. Still, unlike many European cities, there is plenty of opportunity to cool off in air-conditioned restaurants, cafes and stores.

Fall is glorious in the Big Apple. Cool days and crisp nights usher in a new season of Broadway plays, university students and the hustle-bustle of office workers whose summer vacations are mere memories.

Here are the average yearly temperatures in New York City. However, keep in mind that there is nothing average about New York and the temps tend to fluctuate higher or lower:

• January   26(L) 38 (H)
• February   27 (L) 40 (H)
• March   34 (L) 49 (H)
• April   44 (L) 61 (H)

- May   53 (L) 72 (H)
- June   63 (L) 80 (H)
- July   68 (L) 85 (H)
- August   67 (L) 84 (H)
- September   60 (L) 77 (H)
- October   50 (L) 66 (H)
- November   41 (L) 54 (H)
- December   31 (L) 42 (H)

What to Pack

Pack for the season. Your woolies and warmest coats and boots if you'll be visiting in the winter (November through March). Spring is tough: days can warm up but nights cool down so you'll need to layer. Travel here in the summer and your suitcases will be light—shorts, T-shirts, sundresses are all you'll need. Also pack a bathing suit if you decide to escape the heat and head for Long Island's beaches—or if your hotel has as swimming pool.

New York is a casual town. Shorts, jeans, T-shirts, sandals and sneakers, anything goes. If you will be going to the theater pack a city-chic outfit. There are only a handful of restaurants where he'll be required to wear a jacket and tie (and chances are you won't be dining at those with children).

Strollers & Backpacks

New York is a walking town and you'll definitely need a stroller if you've got young kids. Some of my fondest memories of living in Manhattan are taking walks with my son in a stroller. Good news: Most museums allow strollers (although you won't be permitted to bring a stroller into every exhibit within the museum). If you have an infant, pack along a snuggly and keep him or her tucked in front of you. I know a lot of parents love those backpack contraptions that they put their kids into and they're great in some situations. However, in a city setting, I prefer to see my son in front of me so I can keep on eye on him.

Arrivals & Departures

Making Plane Reservations

Thanks to the Web, finding competitive airfares is a cinch. But the choices can be dizzying and airfares change faster than a New York minute.

General rule of thumb: The further out you book the lower the fare. As soon as you know of your children's school vacation schedules try to plan your flights. There is a handful of good websites to tap. Expedia (www.expedia.com), Travelocity (www.travelocity.com) and Orbitz (www.orbitz.com) are good options. Consider flying into a secondary airport (in the case of New York, that would be MacArthur on Long Island or Westchester Airport, both of which are served by major airlines) if you can be flexible with dates. Although not as convenient, it's amazing how drastic the fare can be depending on the date. Of course, you can also visit a specific airline's flight to check out deals and even book your flights. Or call the airline and ask for promotional rates. Connecting flights are usually cheaper but can be tough on families flying with young children. There are a handful of good, no-frills airlines that fly into the metro area, like Song and Jet Blue—their fares are tough to beat (but while they serve New York, they might not fly out of your preferred departure city). Travel agents can be an invaluable resource. A good agent will have preferred-supplier deals with several airlines. You can still surf the Web for good deals. Then, let the agent know of the deal you found and see if he or she can match it or beat it.

Tip: When booking your flight try to determine which side of the airplane will afford fliers with the best skyline view (your travel agent or airline agent may be able to help). Flying over and into Manhattan is a tremendous experience—especially for kids. Fly at night and the city appears as a magical place; during the day it's still a formidable presence. Also, inquire about the best seats at the gate when you arrive at the airport. See if you can change your seats accordingly if it's determined that they'll be better views from the other side of the plane. Remember to smile and pour on the charm and your request might be granted.

Three major airports serve New York City. They are:

John F. Kennedy International Airport (JFK) in Queens, 718/244-4444, www.panynj.com J FK serves primarily international flights, although some domestic flights have arrivals here, too. It is about an hour's drive into midtown Manhattan—*without* traffic.

Fiorello LaGuardia Airport (LGA) in Queens, 718/533-3400, www.panynj.com LaGuardia serves primarily domestic airlines and is the shortest ride into Manhattan—about 35 minutes *without* traffic

Newark Liberty International Airport (EWR) in Newark, New Jersey, 973-961-6000, www.panynj.com Newark serves domestic and international carriers and is about an hour's drive into Manhattan—*without* traffic.

There are two other metropolitan-area airports:

Westchester Airport (HPN) in White Plains, Westchester, New York, 914/995-4860, www.westchestergov.com/airport.

MacArthur Airport (ISP) in Ronkonkoma, Long Island, New York, 631/467-3210, rt.com www.macarthurairport.com.

Here is a sampling of some of the major airlines that serve the New York metropolitan area.
• Delta 800/221-1212, www.delta.com
• American 800/433-7300, www.aa.com

- America West 800/235-9292. www.americawest.com
- Continental 800/525-0280, www.continental.com
- Jet Blue 800/538-2583, www.jetblue.com
- United Airlines 800/241-6522, www.united.com
Song Airlines
- Southwest Airlines 800/435-4322, www.southwest.com
- Virgin Atlantic 800/862-8621, ginatlantic.com www.virginatlantic.com
- US Airways 800/428-4322, www.usair.com

FROM LAGUARDIA TO MANHATTAN

To travel from LaGuardia Airport to midtown Manhattan consider the following children-and-luggage-friendly options:

Taxi

212/NYC-TAXI.

The easiest—and most affordable way—to travel from the airport to Manhattan is by taxi. One fare covers all the passengers in the cab. The metered fare is: $16 to $26 plus bridge and tunnel tolls and tip (the driver usually pays the tunnel or bridge fare at the crossing and then adds it to the final fare). Note: Look for uniformed airport agents who drive yellow medallion taxis. If you follow the signs marked "Ground Transportation" while you exit the airport you'll ultimately find the taxi stand. *(Note: At press time these rates were expected to go up.)*

Gray Line/Express Shuttle USA

800/451-0455, 212/315-3006.

Cost: $13 to $19 one way to midtown Manhattan

This bus will deliver you right to your hotel—but you're not saving money by taking a bus rather than a taxi because a taxi charges per family or load, while the bus charges per person. Still, if you opt for the bus, as you exit the baggage area, go to the Ground Transportation Desk and seek out the Gray Line/Express Shuttle representative who will arrange your service. The bus makes stops at all of the major hotels between 23rd and 63rd streets. Caveat: You may have to wait at the airport but it's not usually more than 20 minutes. Note: When returning to the airport from your Manhattan hotel, you must make reservations for your pickup 24 hours in advance.

FROM JFK TO MANHATTAN
Taxi

212/NYC-TAXI.

As when traveling between New York City and LaGuardia, a yellow medallion taxi is your easiest and most cost-effective bet. As you exit the airport, follow the signs marked "Ground Transportation." Accept rides only from uniformed airport agents. One fare covers all passengers. The fare is $45 flat-fee (non-metered) plus bridge and tunnel tolls and tips.

AirTrain JFK

212/435-7000, www.airtrainjfk.com.

This is an inexpensive way to get to and from Manhattan to JFK ($5 each passenger; children under 5 are free) but it's certainly not the most convenient way. The light rail service makes a 1.8 mile (8 minute) loop linking the nine airline terminals, as well as a 3.3 mile extension with stops at employee parking and long term lots, terminating at Howard Beach subway where you catch the A train (subway) for the ride into Manhattan. Or, you can take it another 3 miles into the Jamaica station and transfer to the Long Island Railroad or the E, J and Z subway lines or a dozen bus lines. Yes, it's a cheaper service but it's not kid-and-luggage friendly by any stretch of the imagination.

FROM NEWARK TO MANHATTAN
Taxi

As when traveling from LaGuardia and JFK, a taxi is the most cost-effective and easiest way to get from Newark International Airport into the City.

Terminal A Taxi: City of Elizabeth Taxi and Limousine Commission, 908-820-4178. Cost: between $40 and $55, plus tolls and tips. There is a $1 charge for each piece of luggage.

Terminals B and C Taxis: City of Newark Taxi and Limousine Commission, 973-733-8912. One fare covers all passengers: the fare ranges between $40 and $55, plus tolls and tips to midtown Manhattan. There is a $1 charge for each piece of luggage over 24 inches.

AirTrain Newark

800/772-3606 or 888/EWR-INFO.

This new, regional rail transportation connects Newark International Airport to Manhattan's Penn Station (33rd Street and Seventh Avenue). Do not follow signs for "Ground Transportation;" instead, look for signs marked "Monorail/AirTrain Link." You can take the AirTrain directly from the arrivals terminal to the Rail Link station and then connect with NJ Transit or Amtrak for rail travel into Penn Station. AirTrain is a free service, but the NJ Transit fare between Newark Airport Station and New York's Penn Station is $11.55.

FROM WESTCHESTER AIRPORT TO MANHATTAN
Taxi/Private Car

914/592-8534.

When you exit the airport look for the signs marked "Ground Transportation." The Limousine Service of Westchester provides by-demand taxi and limo service. Seek out a company representative at the Ground Transportation desk. Cost: $85 plus tolls and tip.

Bee-Line Bus Systems Bus
914/813-7777.
This bus line provides service between the airport and the White Plains train station, at which point you can transfer to a Metro-North train into Grand Central station in midtown Manhattan. The bus service is $1.75 per person, the Metro-North train is about $7 per person (pay no more than $1 for each kid, ages five-to-11-years-old with a fare paying adult; not valid on inbound morning commuting trains). A half-price child fare applies to the fifth child. Kids five years old and under ride free.

FROM MACARTHUR AIRPORT TO MANHATTAN
Shuttle Van and Train
Colonial Transportation (800/464-6900) provides shuttle service between the airport and the Ronkonkoma train station (10 to 12 minute ride), where you can hop aboard a Long Island Railroad train into NYC's Penn Station. Shuttle buses run every 15 to 20 minutes and cost $5 per person. At the airport's entrance (yes, there's one main entrance; it's a small airport), look for a white van marked "Express service between Islip/MacArthur Airport and LIRR/Ronkonkoma Train Station." The train ride is about 1 hour and 20 minutes and the cost is $6.50 to $9.50 depending on whether you'll be traveling at peak times (translation: rush hour). Kids ages five-to-eleven-years-old ride half price; kids five years old and under ride free.

BY PRIVATE CAR & LIMO
Nothing beats the convenience of a private car or limo service from the airport to your hotel. Here are a handful of companies that serve all of the metro airports. You can expect to pay about $25 from LaGuardia, $40 from JFK, $55 from Newark and between $100 and $125 from Westchester and MacArthur airports. Note: You must reserve in advance.
• AAAA Designer Limousine and Transfer Corp., 800/DESIGNER
• Colonial Transportation, 631/589-3500
• Carey Limousine NY 800/336-4646
• Executive Town Car & Limousines, 800/716-2799

BY TRAIN
There are two main train stations in New York City—Pennsylvania Station (on the West Side) and Grand Central Station (on the East Side). Amtrak trains come into both stations, depending on their origin. Penn Station is a final destination for Amtrak's Northeast Corridor routes, including Washington, DC and Boston, MA. This is a great way to travel to New York, and many families

do. The route from Boston and points south to New York is especially pretty as it hugs the coast. Kids 2 years old to 15 travel half-price with an adult; children under 2 years old travel free (not valid on the weekday Acela Express and Metroliner). Student and senior discounts are also offered, and Amtrak offers rail passes available for international travelers. Amtrak also offers train, hotel and attraction packages. Call 800/872-7245, www.amtrak.com.

BY CAR

You won't need—nor want—a car in New York City and if you can get here another way, ditch the car idea. It's expensive to park your car in Manhattan (garage rates average $40 per day) and you won't need it to explore the city and outer boroughs anyway. At all costs, avoid driving into the city at rush hour and on Sunday afternoons in the summer when New Yorkers return from their summer homes in the Hamptons and other leafy or sandy spots. From points north and south, I-95 will take you to New York City, from points west, take I-80. For detailed directions, visit www.mapquest.com or contact AAA if you're a member.

Public Holidays

The City That Never Sleeps gets some shuteye on holidays. But it doesn't enter the REM stage. While offices, government buildings and banks close, many museums and theatres stay open, but check individual listings in the book.

The holidays are:
- **January 1**   New Year's Day
- **Third Monday in January**   Martin Luther King Day
- **Third Monday in February**   President's Day
- **Last Monday in May**   Memorial Day
- **July 4**   Independence Day
- **First Monday in September**   Labor Day
- **Second Monday in October**   Columbus Day
- **November 11**   Veteran's Day/Armistice Day
- **Last Thursday in November**   Thanksgiving
- **December 25**   Christmas

Special Events

In a city as big and diverse as New York, there are special events held every day, from festivals to parades to concerts. For more information about any of them, visit www.nyc.om. Here is a sampling of the major events:

January
- Martin Luther King Day
- National Boat Show at the Jacob Javits Center

February
- Black History Month
- Abraham Lincoln's Birthday
- Chinese New Year Celebrations
- George Washington's Birthday
- New York Yankees Fan Festival
- Westminster Kennel Club Dog Show

March
- St. Patrick's Day
- Ringling Bros. And Barnum & Bailey Circus

April
- Macy's Flower Show
- Central Park Easter Egg Roll
- Fifth Avenue Easter Parade
- Earth Day Celebrations
- Major League Baseball Season Begins
- National Tartan Day Celebration

May
- Cherry Blossom Festival, Brooklyn Botanic Garden
- Tribeca Film Festival
- Memorial Day

Summer (June, July, August)
- Museum Mile Festival (*every second Tuesday in June, rain or shine*)
- Upper East Side National Puerto Rico Day Parade
- JVC Jazz Festival New York
- Shakespeare in the Park at the Delacorte Theater
- Central Park SummerStage
- New York Philharmonic Concerts in the Park
- Bryant Park Film Festival
- Fleet Week
- South Street Seaport Fourth of July Festival
- Macy's Fourth of July Fireworks
- Lincoln Center Out-of-Doors Festival
- Harlem Week
- Midsummer Night Swing at Lincoln Center
- Mostly Mozart Jazz Festival
- U.S. Open Tennis Tournament
- National Puerto Rican Day Parade
- Lesbian and Gay Pride Parade

September
- West Indian American Day Parade, Labor Day
- Feast of San Gennaro in Little Italy
- New York is Book Country Festival
- The New York Film Festival

October
- Greenwich Village Halloween Parade
- New York Rangers Hockey season begins
- New York Knicks Basketball season begins

November
- New York City Marathon
- Veteran's Day Parade
- Thanksgiving Day Parade

December
- Kwanzaa Fest
- Lighting of the bigger-than-life Chanukah Menorah at Fifth Avenue and 59th Street
- Lighting of the Rockefeller Center Christmas tree
- New Year's Eve at Times Square, ball-dropping countdown

Getting Around New York City

There are five boroughs in New York City—the Bronx, Brooklyn, Manhattan, Queens and Staten Island. A lanky necklace of bridges and tunnels links the five boroughs.

Manhattan is an island, flanked on the West Side by the Hudson River and on the East Side by the Harlem River (to the north) and the East River (to the south). North of Manhattan is the Bronx, which is on the mainland. The boroughs of Queens and Brooklyn are located on the western tip of Long Island.

The island of Manhattan is 13.4 miles long and 2.3 miles wide at its widest point.

The streets run east to west and are numbered, ascending in numerical order traveling north from Houston Street all the way up to 220th Street. The streets south of Houston Street have their own names. On average, 20 north-south blocks equal a mile.

Avenues run North to South, beginning with 1st Avenue on the East Side and ending with 12th Avenue on the West Side. Note: Sixth Avenue is also called Avenue of the Americas. The East and West sides of Manhattan are divided by Fifth Avenue. The farther you travel from Fifth Avenue the higher the numbers; there are roughly 100 street addresses per block.

Broadway is the only avenue that cuts diagonally through the city and runs in some form from Manhattan's southern tip all the way to the state capital, Albany, about 150 miles away.

The city is sectioned into regions.

- Anything below 1st Street in Greenwich Village is considered **Downtown**.
- The area between 1st and 14th Streets is considered **The Village**. The neighborhood west of Broadway is considered Greenwich Village and the neighborhood east of Broadway is considered the East Village.
- The area between 14th and 34th Streets, west of Broadway, is known as **Chelsea**.
- Between 34th and 59th Streets is **Midtown**.
- From 59th to 110th Streets is where you'll find the **Upper West Side** and the **Upper East Side**. Between the two "sides" lies **Central Park**.
- The neighborhood between 110th and 145th Streets is **Harlem**.
- The area between 145th to 220th Streets contains the neighborhoods of **Washington Heights**.

Generally speaking, the traffic patterns are as follows: one-way going east on even-numbered streets and one-way going west on odd-numbered streets. Main streets that run east west are two-way yet some of the smaller streets are the exception to this rule.

Orient yourself further by logging onto www.nycvisit.com to download maps. Or, visit one of the visitor information kiosks located throughout town. And keep in mind, that New Yorkers are friendly and love to share their knowledge of the City with tourists. Don't be shy—just ask.

BY CAR

Are you kidding? You don't want to get behind the wheel to drive around the city. End of story.

Car Rental

Again, you won't need—or want—a car to explore the city, however you may want to rent one to explore the suburbs. Here is a listing of car rental agencies in Manhattan.

- Dollar 800/800/3665, www.dollar.com
- Budget 800/527-0700, www.budget.com
- National 800/227-7368, www.nationalcar.com
- Hertz 800/654-3131, www.hertz.com
- Enterprise 800/736-8222, www.enterprise.com
- Avis 800/917-2847, www.avis.com

BY SUBWAY & BUS

See map on inside front cover for the Manhattan portion of the subway.

A whopping 3.5 million people rely on New York's subway and bus system on a daily basis. Many of the subway and bus lines operate 24 hours a day. The fare is $2, even if you're only going one stop—it is the same as if you're taking it to the end of the route.

You'll need a MetroCard to use the subway, but you can also use change for the buses. Best bet: Purchase an unlimited-ride card for one day (the Fun Pass $7), seven day card ($21) or, if you'll be in town for an extended vacation (lucky you) a 30 day care ($70). You can buy pay-per-ride cards in increments of $2 to $80. If you buy a pay-per-ride card worth $10 or more, you get a 20 percent bonus. Note: You can use your Metrocard for free transfers between buses and subways or bus-to-bus within two hours of the ride's start.

You can buy MetroCards at any subway station, hotels, and newsstands throughout the city. You can also purchase a MetroCard at NYC's Official Visitor Information Center.

Note: The subway is safe and reliable—but you should stay away from the subway late at night and opt to take a cab or bus instead.

BY TAXI

How to hail a cab: Standing at the curb (on the sidewalk,) simply hold your arm out and wave. (Kids love to do this but make sure they stay on the curb). You can hail a yellow taxi on any street or at taxi stands at most major hotels. Look for the middle section of the taxi's roof light to be on. If its' not, and the off-duty lights are on (on each end of the light) or, if no part of the light is lighted, the taxi won't stop because it already has another passenger or is off-duty. Tip: Hail a cab that is headed in the direction you want to go. Also, make sure it is a yellow taxi; if it is not, you risk being overcharged.

BY WATER TAXI

You can circumvent the congested New York streets and jump aboard a bright yellow water catamaran taxi instead. The 74-passenger-capacity taxis zip along the rivers serving neighborhoods, parks and attractions along the West Side, Lower Manhattan and Downtown Brooklyn waterfronts. Bonus: There's even a café onboard. One-stop tickets cost $4 (for all ages) and a one-way ticket (if you'll be going one way for more than one stop) costs $8 adults, $6 seniors and kids 12 years old and younger. Bonus: Buy a one-day pass, which allows you to hop on and off New York Water Taxi at any time during a 24 hour period for $15 adults, $12 seniors (65 years and older) and kids (12 years old and under).

Note: Children two years old and under ride free. Note: Babies in baby strollers are allowed; strollers with no babies are not. You can purchase tickets aboard the boats, at one of the kiosks (seasonal) and at some of the landing docks. The taxis operate year-round, rain or snow. For more information, call 212/742-1969 or visit www.nywatertaxi.com.

BY ORGANIZED BUS TOURS
Gray Line New York Sightseeing/Coach USA
800/669-0051 or 212/445-0848, www.newyorksightseeing.com.

Kids and adults love the double-decker bus tours—the beauty of which, you can jump on and off as you please for two consecutive days.

Showbiz Insiders Tour
800/669-0051 or 212/445-0848 (Reservations are required, you can also buy them online). www.newyorksightseeing.com.

A Gray Line tour of the country's hit television and Broadway productions, this tour allows star-struck visitors a chance to enter the stage door at the *Lion King*'s New Amsterdam Theatre and to meet a Rockette at Radio City Music Hall. After a lunch at Planet Hollywood in Times Square, the tour culminates with a performance by a current Broadway actor at Gray Line New York Sightseeing's private theater. Bonus: Opportunities for autographs and photographs with the stars.

Harlem Spirituals/New York Visions
212/391-0900, www.harlemspirituals.com.

Gospel music and jazz are part of this company's MO. Tours are offered of Manhattan, the Bronx and Brooklyn.

Harlem Your Way! Tours Unlimited
800/382-9363, www.harlemyourwaytours.com.

General tour of Harlem (jazz, gospel, architecture, and churches), as well as customized tours, including special children's tours.

New York Movie Tours
888/MOVIE-TOUR, www.newyorkmovie.tours.com.

Visit famous movie locations around New York. Kids and teens will know some of the flicks, including *Ghostbusters* and *Men in Black*.

Shop Gotham Shopping Tours
www.shopgotham.com.

One of the Big Apple's newest tours, this tour is designed for your teenager daughter who loves to shop Bonus: Take the tour and receive a discount card good for a 10 to 20 percent reduction at boutiques or a list of sample sales and events.

On Location Tours, Inc.

212/209-3370, www.sceneontv.com.

Calling all couch potatoes. Grab a seat on one of these bus tours of famous TV and movie sites. You can choose from the following:

Manhattan, TV and Movie Tour, which includes *Friends, Seinfeld, Spiderman* and *You've Got Mail;* Sex and the City Tour, including 35 spots in the series, such as Carrie's apartment; the Sopranos' Tour, which features 40 sites; and the Central Park Movie Tour, which covers 60 locations.

Kramer's Reality Tour

800/KRAMERS, www.kennykramer.com.

Seinfeld is the quintessential New York story and this three-hour coach bus tour takes a behind-the-scenes look.

BY BOAT
Circle Line Sightseeing Cruises

Pier 83, West 42nd Street and 12th Avenue, 212/563-3200, www.circleline42.com.

Circle Line is one of the city's most established lines to operate cruises around Manhattan. There is a three-hour narrated Full Island Cruise, which is not the one you want if you have small kids or impatient teens (ahem). The two-hour Semi-Circle Cruise or evening two-hour Harbor Lights Cruise (the skyline at night is a jewel to behold) is a better bet.

Even better though for kids, is the *Beast*—a 30-minute thrill ride that is not for the faint of heart. This boat, which departs from Pier 83 at West 42nd Street, zips along the river and kids adore it! For information about the Beast, visit www.infocl@circleline.com. Note: Kids must be over 40 inches tall or five years old. Cost: From mid-May to the end of September, open daily, noon to dusk; Adults $16, kids (5 to 12 years old) $10. Note: During the month of October open only on Saturday and Sunday. The boat departs every hour on the hour.

Circle Line also operates the new Circle Line Statue of Liberty Ferry/*Zephyr*, a luxury catamaran of Battery Park. 212/269-5755, www.zephyrcruises.com. There's a kid-friendly, one-hour narrated tour of just the Statue of Liberty and Ellis Island Immigration Museum.

Chelsea Screamer

212/924-6262, www.chelseascreamer.com.

We were hanging out at Chelsea Piers one day after work and camp (my son was 7) and saw a group of people lined up for the *Screamer*, which was new at the time. We signed on and what a blast we had. We got wet—it was a warm summer night so that was okay—as the boat zipped along the East River past the Brooklyn Bridge, the Statue of Liberty, Ellis Island, up to the Intrepid and back. The trip takes about 30 minutes. We had such a good time that we made plans to take my mother on the boat the following week. She reminded us that she takes Dramamine for canoe rides and we decided this wasn't the cruise for her. Or for anyone in your family if they're prone to seasickness. The boat travels at a good clip—about 45 mph. Our guide was a scream, cracking jokes while dishing up important and trivial facts about the City. The Screamer is for kids ages of all ages, while the *Beast* (see Circle Line tours) is better suited for teens. Operates May through October.

Cost: $15 adults, $8 kids 12 years old and under, and free kids under two years old. Pier 62 at Chelsea Piers (West 23rd Street and Hudson River).

The Pioneer

212/748-8590, www.southstreetseaport.org.

It's pricier than some of the other "tours" ($25 adults, $20 students and seniors, $15 children 12 years old and younger), but a two-hour sightseeing cruise aboard this historic schooner is a magical experience. Departs from South Street Seaport several times a day.

Staten Island Ferry

718/815-BOAT, www.siferry.com.

A great way to see the Manhattan skyline, New York harbor and the Statue of Liberty—for free. The ferry runs 24 hours a day between St. George on Staten Island and Whitehall Street in Manhattan. The five-mile trip is about 25 minutes each way. More than 70,000 passengers use the ferry each day.

NY Waterway Baseball Cruises

800/533-3779, www.nywaterway.com.

Hit a home run with the baseball nut in your family with this cruise to Yankee Stadium and Shea Stadium. Bonus: Packages are available, including tickets to games. Round-trip fares are $17 adults, $14 seniors, $13 kids under 12.

BY FOOT
ARTime

718/797-1573.

Kid-friendly tour for kids in the range of five to ten years old. Tours run seasonally. Call for more information.

Museum Adventures

212/794-2867, www.museumadventuresnyc.com.

For kids (and their parents) tours that include visits of museums throughout the city. Each tour culminates with an art activity.

Big Onion Walking Tours

212/439-1090, www.bigonion.com.

Year-round tours of New York's historic districts and ethnic neighborhoods led by "smart" tour guides (the company insists they all hold advanced degrees in American history or related fields), and are licensed by the city. The annual Christmas Eve stroll through Greenwich Village is magical and includes a reading of *'Twas the Night Before Christmas.*

Central Park Conservancy

212/360-2726, rknyc.org www.centralparknyc.org.

You can choose from eight different walking tours of Central Park. The tours span woodlands and meadows, bridges and waterways and offer snippets of info about Central Park's history and design. Highlight: One-hour tours written and led by NYC teens. Bonus: All tours are free. No reservations required.

Cityhunt Urban Adventures

212/696-6537, www.cityhunt.org.

Think scavenger hunt and you get the picture.

Joyce Gold History Tours of NY

212/242-5762, www.nyctours.com.

Bus and walking tours that skip along with interesting commentary of the city's history and architecture, a Joyce Gold tour is one of the City's most popular tours. A teacher of NY history at a local college, Ms. Gold is a fountain of information. Note: These tours are geared primarily toward adults.

Grand Central Terminal Tours

212/883-2420, www.grandcentralterminal.com.

Two free walking tours are offered of this magnificent terminal building. On Wednesdays, the Municipal Arts Society runs a tour; meet at 12:30 pm at the information booth on the Grand Concourse (212/935-3960). On Fridays, a tour is conducted by the Grand Central Partnership; meet at 12:30 pm in front of the Philip Morris/Whitney Museum across the street from the terminal (212/697-1245). (For more specific information about Grand Central Station, check out the separate listing in the midtown section of the book).

Toro Associates, Inc.

212/625-9977, www.chinatowninfo.com.

A $10 walking tour that gives you a sneak peek into Chinatown's historical landmarks, herbal medicine stores and jade and crystal shops.

Big Apple Greeter

212/669-8159, www.bigapplegreeter.org.

Explore Manhattan for free with volunteer guides who'll meet you at your hotel or wherever you want and give you an intimate peek at the city (any borough)—by foot, subway or bus. The tours generally run two-to-four hours. Over 500 New Yorkers volunteers are trained to lead these guides; tours are conducted in over 30 languages. Bonus: All tours are free. Note: Reserve at least a month in advance.

BY BIKE
Bite of the Apple Tours/Central Park Bike Tours
2 Columbus Circle/Broadway at 59th Street, 212/541-8759. www.centralparkbiketour.com.
Leisurely two-hour bike rides through Central Park. Tip: If your kids love the movies, sign up for the Central Park Movie Scenes Bike Tour. Cost: $35 adults, $20 kids 15 years old and under.

Bike the Big Apple
201/837-1133, www.bikethebigapple.com.
These two-to-five-hour cycling tours take visitors over bridges, on quiet, ethnic streets and places not generally seen on traditional tours. Yes, kids take these tours—there's a guide to lead the group and a guide following. The pace is slow and all skill levels participate. You can also customize a tour for your family: $20 per hour, per person with a minimum two people. Tours include bicycle and helmet. Cost: About $69 per person.

BY AIR
Helicopter Flight Services
212/355-08011, www.heliny.com.
Don't forget your cameras for the fabulous aerial views. The 13-to- 15-minute New Yorker Tour soars over the Statue of Liberty, Empire State Building, and Intrepid Aircraft Carrier. Cost: $109 per person.

Liberty Helicopters, Inc.
212/967-2099, www.libertyhelicopters.com.
Five-to-seven minute tours that sweep over The Empire State Building, the Intrepid and Central Park. Cost: $56 per person.

Parent Tip
Many cities in the U.S. have Duck Tours and kids love them. New York City isn't one of them. Just the thought of one of the oversized amphibious vehicles navigating the congested, taxi-honking streets of New York City at rush hour is a vision that brings a smile. We promise, though, that a New York City taxi ride can be just as exciting—if not more.

☙

New York City Neighborhoods

Lower Manhattan

Unfortunately, the southernmost tip of Manhattan is etched in most of the world's memory as the tragic spot where the devastating act of terrorism hit on 9/11. Many tourists to this part of town come to view the **World Trade Center site** and to pay their respects to the heroes who lost their lives here. Make no mistake about it though, lower Manhattan is still the financial center of the world: **The New York Stock Exchange** is here, as is the Federal Reserve Bank. And it's also home to **South Street Seaport** and **Battery Park City**.

Little Italy/NoLita/Chinatown

Little Italy isn't the same as when I lived on nearby Sullivan Street in Soho and would walk the couple of blocks to Little Italy for my pick of a great Italian meal at a lively neighborhood restaurant. It's lost some of its ethnicity in recent years as a result of residents moving out to say *bon giorno* to the suburbs (think *Sopranos*). But it's still a fun spot to visit. Of course the best reason to visit Little Italy (not unlike Italy itself) is the food. Narrow streets like **Mott** and **Mulberry** are flanked with a handful of good Italian restaurants, though not nearly as many in year's gone by. If you're in town in September you're in for an Italian treat: the **San Gennaro Festival** takes over Little Italy with sausage and peppers, zepoles, cannolis, and festive lights and music.

Chinatown is the largest Chinese community in the Western Hemisphere, a vibrant, colorful neighborhood with lots of buzz and activity. Tourists—and New Yorkers—love Chinatown for a great meal of dim sum. Chinatown is also the spot to snag a street bargain. My son's older sister, Jessica, loves to scour Chinatown's streets for handbag knockoffs. Chinatown is also tons of fun during the **Chinese New Year**. Fireworks used to explode but have been banned in recent years. Still, parades of dragons snake through the narrow streets, and everybody has a good time.

NoLita stands for North of Little Italy, and it's where you can stroll and search for the kind of off-beat merchandise you won't find in upscale boutiques uptown such as unique embroidered purses, hand-crafted boots and interesting jewelry pieces.

Lower East Side

While the rest of Manhattan moves in a New York minute, the Lower East Side moves a bit slower. In the 1800's, the Lower East Side was a gateway slum for new immigrants and you should visit the **Lower East Side Tenement Museum** to get a taste of what it used to be like. This is a fascinating museum for kids. **Orchard Street** is a hot spot for bargain shopping. There is also a handful of ethnic eateries like **Katz's Delicatessen** where stacked corned beef sandwiches are the rule, and pickles and knish spots.

Soho/Noho/Tribeca/Greenwich Village/East Village

Soho (which stands for South of Houston Street) has come a long way from the days of loft-living artists and quiet neighborhood streets, thanks to the infusion of trendy boutiques and restaurants. Some people, especially jaded New Yorkers think it's come *too* far along—at the expense of the neighborhood's once artsy flair. Yes, there has been a proliferation of shops that you'd find in Anywhere U.S.A. But having once lived in Soho, I can tell you that this is still very much a neighborhood with mom and pop shops like **Joe's Dairy** on Sullivan Street. Joe's makes and sells the best mozzarella anywhere in the City. Stop in and get some fresh out of the oven. The art scene is still very much alive in Soho, with an estimated 250 art galleries alone. The moral of this tale is that if you seek you shall find the fabric of Soho of days past.

NoHo (which stands for North of Houston Street) is a relatively new neighborhood with some trendy restaurants and stores. And Tribeca, which stands for Triangle Below Canal Street, is home to a handful of hip restaurants, cool shops and loft apartments (John F. Kennedy Jr. and Carolyn Bissette lived here). However, NoHo and Tribeca don't have near the number of shops and restaurants and tourists that Soho does.

Greenwich Village has always been a bohemian mix of unique shops, cafes, bookstores, jazz clubs, off-off Broadway theaters and it still is. Teens especially love to spend time down here (think body piercing, dyed hair, spiked hair, grunge jeans and you've got the makings for a teen dream-come-true.) **Washington Square Park** is a lively concrete-and-grassy-square that's popular with nearby NYU students—there's always something or someone interesting to see.

The East Village has a rep as a really far out, progressive neighborhood. It probably isn't the spot for a Sunday brunch with grandma (unless your last name is Osbourne), but your 15 year old will think it's totally bad (that's a good thing.) Rebellious teens especially love this part of the City with its salty edge—in fact, it makes Greenwich Village look like Parochial school.

Flatiron District

Named for the really interesting-shaped, brick-and-limestone **Flatiron Building** at 23rd St. and Broadway (you'll know it when you see it, it's the building that's shaped like an iron), this area is architecturally stunning. The Flatiron District is home to one of the City's best playgrounds and kid-friendly parks, **Madison Square Park**. And **Union Square**, home to the popular **Greenmarket**, where New Yorkers buy fresh, farm produce, is also here.

Gramercy Park

A chic, tree-lined residential neighborhood with a gated (key, please) park. There are a couple of great restaurants and shops in the Gramercy Park neighborhood, but it's primarily a residential part of town.

Murray Hill

Another residential section of the City with little else going on—and the people who live here wouldn't want it any other way. (Technically, the Empire State Building is in Murray Hill, but it's really more of a midtown location).

Chelsea

Not too long ago, Chelsea was an invisible neighborhood, with not much to offer in the way of culture, dining or nightlife. It's on the map now, thanks in part to the sprawling and ambitious **Chelsea Piers Sports Complex** and the many art galleries, cafes and boutiques. It's also home to the city's gay population, who moved uptown from the Village.

Clinton

Just to the north of Chelsea, this neighborhood was once known as Hell's Kitchen (translation: porn shops, seedy apartments). It's been cleaned up, "renamed" and, while still not the most desirable of addresses in town, it's come a long way.

Theater District/Times Square

This celebrated New York neighborhood, once seedy and scary, now is one of the city's most popular tourist spots—for kids! **Toy's 'R Us** opened an enormous store here, complete with indoor Ferris wheel. A handful of hotels and restaurants (**ESPN Zone** scores big) have super transformed **Times Square** with more neon, blinking lights and action than ever. Times Square is where it's at.

Midtown

Skyscraper office buildings, chic restaurants and city landmarks are what this part of town is all about. During the holidays, midtown is packed with tourists who stroll Fifth Avenue to admire the holiday displays and the illustrious tree at Rockefeller Center. Midtown is also where you'll find the highest concentration of hotels (although Times Square is catching up), Grand Central Station and, to the east, the United Nations.

Upper East Side

Manhattan's most upscale and expensive neighborhood is where you'll discover an impressive collection of museums, boutiques, trendy restaurants, and elegant townhouse mansions, especially along lovely **Madison Avenue**.

Stroll this neighborhood on a weekday morning or afternoon and you'll see lots of nannies pushing Cadillac strollers and socialites dining on *foie gras* at outdoor cafes. The Upper East Side is noticeably quieter than the Upper West—there's not as much traffic and less horn honking (relatively speaking).

Note: There is no subway that runs from the Upper East to the Upper West sides; Central Park divides the two. Your best bet: Take the **cross-town bus** at 79th or 86th streets, or walk across the Park.

Central Park

The heart and soul of New York City, Central Park is a breath of fresh air—literally and figuratively speaking. It's an 843-acre backyard for New Yorkers who dwell in small, cramped apartments. They come to bike, jog, stroll, walk their dogs, have a picnic, listen to outdoor concerts, blow off steam…Central Park also tugs at the hearts of tourists with its scenic skyline views, it's rambling paths, grassy lawns and, that famous restaurant, **Tavern on the Green**.

Upper West Side

Manhattan's Upper West is funkier and artier than the Upper East. While stockbrokers and real estate moguls tend to live on the Upper East, writers, editors, dancers, actors and musicians opt for the Upper West. The **American Museum of Natural History** is a magnet for families—this is the most popular museum for kids in the city. You'll also discover **Lincoln Center**, the largest cultural complex in the world, and the new, swanky **Time Warner Center** in this part of town.

Morningside Heights

The neighborhood above Central Park (to the west) lies this busy part of town, home to **Columbia University**, the **Cathedral of St. John the Divine** (the Blessings of the Animals service is not to be missed) and **Riverside Church**, another glorious landmark.

Harlem/Washington Heights

Once down and out, Harlem is on the map as a hip place to be. The neighborhood has a jazzy past (jazz artists like Count Bassie, Duke Ellington and Dizzy Gillepsie used to play in clubs here), and it's still the place to hear great music from gospel to jazz. Bill Clinton made news when he chose to rent office space here. Also, a number of popular, trendy stores have opened in Harlem. But in the midst of the gentrification, Harlem has retained its soul and spirituality. Travel way north to Washington Heights and you'll come to **The Cloisters** in Fort Tyron Park with pretty views of the Hudson and great medieval art.

The Bronx

While the Bronx bombers might think the curse of Babe Ruth is one theory for the Yankees success, residents up here think it's the Bronx that's the lucky charm. **Yankee Stadium** is one great reason to visit the Bronx. But there are others, like the **Bronx Zoo** and the **New York Botanical Garden**.

Queens

The temporary, two-year relocation of Manhattan's **MOMA** (Museum of Modern Art) to Long Island City here (while the midtown location underwent an extensive facelift) put this diverse neighborhood—directly to the east of the City—on the map as a tourist destination. Queens is also extremely ethnically diverse, with pockets of Indian, Jamaicans, Greek, Chinese, Korean and other neighborhoods rich in ethnicity scattered throughout.

Staten Island

Really closer to New Jersey than the City, Staten Island is home to many commuters who make the daily ride on the Staten Island ferry into lower Manhattan. There are a handful of attractions (**Staten Island Children's Museum** and **Staten Island Zoo**). Not many tourists visit Staten Island though—but a free ride on the **Staten Island Ferry** is tourist must-do.

Brooklyn

Brooklyn is one of my favorite neighborhoods, and has been a favorite spot of writers for decades (Walt Whitman and Arthur Miller lived here). There are also tremendous views of downtown Manhattan from the **Brooklyn Promenade**. And **DUMBO** (Down Under the Manhattan Bridge Overpass) has given Brooklyn a new edge with artsy events and trendy eateries. All said, Brooklyn is Manhattan—centuries ago. Used to be that people who worked in Manhattan opted to live in Brooklyn, thanks to cheaper rents. Not anymore. Finding an affordable apartment in the nice sections of Brooklyn (Brooklyn Heights, Cobble Hill, Park Slope) is no less competitive than trying to secure one across the bridge in the big city.

When visiting Manhattan, do make the time to walk across the **Brooklyn Bridge**—a stunning, one-mile long suspension bridge that took almost two decades to build. A tourist must-do.

Playgrounds, Parks, Gardens & Recreation

New York City has more than 1,700 parks, playgrounds and recreation areas in five boroughs. Here is a sampling of some of the best of them; you'll undoubtedly stumble across others on your own.

NATURE CENTERS, PARKS & GARDENS
Battery Park City Parks Conservancy (BPCPC)

2 South End Avenue, 212/267-9700, www.bpcparks.org.

Roughly 32 acres dotted with playing fields and playgrounds make the parks and gardens along this stretch the pride and joy of downtown Manhattan. Designed and maintained (without the use of toxic chemicals) by celebrated landscape architects and artists, Battery Park also contains more than two-dozen art installations, four museums and several restaurants.

Shadowed by soaring skyscrapers, this is the spot for free weekly recreation, art and sports activities for kids of all ages during the spring, summer and fall months. Wagner Park, located at the southern tip of Battery City Park, is a perfect place here to spy the Statue of Liberty and Ellis Island.

Rockefeller Park, also part of the BPCPC, is a sliver of a park, with wide expansive lawns for hanging and picnicking with a little bit of everything within a gated area: a sculpture garden for kids, a wading pool, a playground and a carousel. There's also a stretch of grass to picnic on and an esplanade for biking and rollerblading. The playground is particularly popular. On a hot day kids can run through elephant and hippopotamus sprinklers. There are several sand play areas, and a huge net, rope and chain bridge. Of course there are the requisite swings and you can also rent board games, ping pong paddles, jump ropes and balls at the Park House. For older kids there's a basketball and handball court.

East River Park

Along the FDR Drive, beginning at Montgomery Street up to 14th Street.

A park for sports enthusiasts with fields for soccer, football, softball and baseball. Bonus: Great views of the East River and the Brooklyn and Manhattan bridges.

Central Park

(see separate chapter)

Brooklyn Botanic Garden

900 Washington Avenue (Eastern Parkway), Brooklyn, 718/623-7200. www.bbg.org. Open Tuesday through Sunday 10am to 6pm, closed Mondays (except holidays). Admission: students $3, seniors $5, kids 16 and under free. Free to everyone Saturdays 10am to noon, all day Tuesday; seniors free Tuesday and Friday.

This 52-acre gem blooms with specialty gardens, including an amazing Japanese cherry blossom festival each spring that culminates in a splash of pink-and-white. The Sakura Matsuri festival celebrates the flowering of the Kanzan cherry trees on the Garden's Cherry Esplanade, as well as about three dozen other varieties of Japanese cherry. Bonus: Japanese food is available during the festival. Note: The festival is held rain or shine.

Staten Island Botanical Garden

1000 Richmond Terrace (Tysen Street to Snug Harbor Road), Staten Island, 718/273-8200, www.sibg.org. Open: Dawn to dusk. Closed Monday. Admission: Free. Chinese Scholar's Garden free Tuesday from 10am to 1pm; other times $5 adults, $4 students, seniors and kids 12 years old and under.

There are 50 acres with 25 gardens on the grounds of the Snug Harbor Cultural Center. The Chinese Scholar's Garden has lovely reflecting pools and meditation courtyards.

Queens Botanical Gardens

43-50 Main Street (Elder Avenue), Flushing, Queens 718 886 3800, www.queensbotanical.org. Open: Closed Monday (except holidays). Spring and summer hours: During the month of March, the gardens are open Tuesday through Sunday 8 am to 4:30 pm. The months of April through September, the gardens are open Tuesday through Friday 8 am to 6 pm and Saturday and Sunday 8 am to 7 pm. Admission: Free.

Thirty-nine acres with formal gardens, this spot started out as a 1939 World's Fair exhibit. If you're going to visit only one botanical garden while in town, this isn't the one—not that there's anything wrong with it, but the New York Botanical Garden *(see next listing)* or Brooklyn Botanic Gardens are better bets.

New York Botanical Garden

200th Street and Southern Boulevard (Kazimiroff Blvd), Bronx, 718/817-8777, www.nybg.org. Open: Tuesday through Sunday and holidays, 10am to 6pm (November through March open until 5pm). Closed Monday except holidays. Cost: Combo tickets are Adults $13, seniors and students $11, kids under 12 years old $5, and kids two and under. Tickets for grounds admission only are Adults, $6, seniors $3, students $2, kids years old and under are free. Note: Free admission Saturday 10am to noon, and all day Wednesday.

A 250-acre paradise in the Bronx, this jewel is a National Historic Landmark. It boasts 27 outdoor gardens and plant collections and the Enid A. Haupt Conservatory, a Victorian conservatory with a huge 90-foot-high glass dome. The Everett Children's Adventure Garden, 12 acres of gardens and wetlands, will make any kid a green thumb with hands-on plant discovery activities; there's also a picnic area.

Flushing Meadows-Corona Park

Long Island Expressway—Roosevelt Avenue, Van Wyck Expressway—111th St., Queens, 718/760-6565, www.nycgovparks.org. Open: Seven days a week dawn to dusk. Admission: Free

Home to the 1939 and 1964 World's Fairs, Flushing Meadows has an ambitious selection of recreational activities (see individual listings), as well as a botanical garden.

Riverbank State Park

145th Street (at the Hudson River), 212/694-3600, www.nysparks.com. Open: Seven days a week, dawn to dusk Admission: Free.

A 28-acre oasis near Columbia University, Riverbank has a pedestrian esplanade, as well as a carousel (open only on Saturdays and Sundays during warm weather months; 50 cents). There are also tennis courts, an outdoor ice-skating rink and an Olympic sized indoor pool. Note: No bicycles allowed.

Parent Tip
Where in the world is the statue of Balto? It's located just inside Central Park at 67th Street and 5th Avenue.

PLAYGROUNDS
You could argue that New York City is a giant playground for people of all ages and countries and you'd be right. There are tons of fun diversions and activities. But for the purposes of this section, we're talking the sandy type of playgrounds for kids under 12 years old.

Some of these playgrounds are located in parks with benches that lure office workers to enjoy their lunch—making for a complete New York scene. For instance, on a pretty day, the Madison Square Park Playground located in the shadows of the Flatiron building, is a magnet for the stroller crowd, as well as professionals with their sleeves rolled up, ties tucked in, munching on lunch. There are way too many playgrounds to list in these pages.

Here is a listing of some of the best, strategically placed play spots to swing, slide and chill:
- **West 67th Street Playground,** North of Tavern on the Green
- **Heckscher Playground,** West 62nd Street
- **Diana Ross Playground,** West 81st Street (Central Park)
- **Hudson Street Playground**
- **West 84th Street Playground**

Parent Tip
Ancient Playground East , 85th Street and Fifth Avenue.
Combine a visit to the Metropolitan Museum with this popular playground. Fashioned after the Egyptian Wing of the Metropolitan Museum, which is located next door, this outdoor spot is one of the few playgrounds that doesn't just cater to the diaper crowd. Rope and tire swings, pyramids and a chain-link bridge entertain older kids, while bucket swings and a sandbox engage younger kids. (Don't let them dig too deep, they might just excavate a mummy.) Teens might like the chess and checker tables.

- **Spector Playground,** West 85th Street
- **Safari Playground,** West 91 Street
- **Tompkins Square Park,** Avenue A and 7th Street and Avenue B and 10th Street
- **Wild West Playground,** West 93rd Street
- **Pat Hoffman Friedman Playground,** East 79th Street (Central Park)
- **Pier 51 Playground at Horatio Street**

BASKETBALL

New York is a hoops town and you'll see pick-up games all around town. Even if your kids don't live for the game, you'll want to spend at least a couple of minutes at "The Cage," basketball courts at Sixth Avenue and West 4th Street. You'll know you arrived by the crowds of on-lookers watching the action with mouth-gaping awe. We've spent several summer evenings licking ice cream cones while admiring these hoopsters in action. Some of the kids who play pick-up games here are serious NBA contenders. Yes, your kids can join in but they'd better be good. A wiser bet for joining a pick-up game: St. Catherine's Playground on First Avenue between 67th and 68th Streets. Or, if you're milling about the Great Lawn in Central Park (around 85th Street), they might be able to get in on the action at the nearby courts.

Parent Tip

If your kids are sports-enthusiasts, they'll most likely want to jump, run, hit and slam-dunk while on vacation. But you certainly don't want to lug basketballs, tennis rackets and baseball bats to town. Don't sweat it. You have several choices.

At Central Park's **North Meadow Recreation Center,** located mid-park at 97th Street, there are handball courts, indoor and outdoor climbing walls, basketball courts and a fitness learning center and you can borrow equipment (with ID) like Double Dutch jump ropes. Call 212/ 348-4867 ext. 10, www.centralparknyc.org

Chelsea Pier Field House (Pier 62 at Chelsea Piers) is another hot spot for athletic kids. You can rent playing time on a basketball court or slug baseballs in the batting cage. (See Chelsea Piers entry for more information.)

BIKING

Central Park is fun for cyclists of all ages—if your last name is Knievel. Seriously, you must be alert to dodging in-line skaters, joggers and oblivious strollers. You can rent bicycles mid-park at the Loeb Boathouse.

The most family-friendly stretch is along Riverside Park, thanks to its relatively flat and wide paths from about 83rd street up to 96th.

You can also bike over the Brooklyn Bridge which is really cool—just be sure to stay in the bike "lanes"; pedestrians have their own lane, but these lanes are not clearly marked, there's little signage and things can get dicey.

The Hudson River bike path is ambitious, spanning from Battery Park at the southern tip of Manhattan all the way up to the George Washington Bridge. Caveat: There are some stretches along the way that are difficult to maneuver, especially way uptown.

BOWLING

For bowling-loving families, there are a couple of popular bowling spots in town but you'll note they're probably considerably more expensive than bowling in your hometown.

Bowlmor Lanes

110 University Place (between 12th and 13th streets), 212/255-8188. Cost: Monday through Friday before 5pm, $6.45 per person per game, Saturday before 5 pm and all day Sunday $8.45 per person per game (nobody under 21 years old is allowed at night).

A hip, happening, date-night spot that's family-friendly during the day with 42 lanes, automatic scoring and gutter bumpers to keep the balls from going astray.

Chelsea Piers AMF Bowling

Located between Pier 59 and 60 at West 23rd Street and the Hudson River, 212/835-2695, www.chelseapiersbowl.com. Cost: $7.50 per game per person daily, plus $4.50 equipment rental per person. After 9 pm, anybody 21 years old and under must be accompanied by an adult.

New York families love to bowl here. It's clean and has gutter bumpers. Bonus: You can order food from the restaurant and they'll deliver it to your lane.

Leisure Time Bowling

625 Eighth Avenue (in the Port Authority Bus Terminal) on the second level, 212/268-6909. Cost: $6 per person, per game ($7 Thursday through Sunday after 5 pm). Shoe rental is extra.

Even seasoned New Yorkers will look at you as if you have ten heads if you ask for directions to the bowling alley in the Port Authority Bus Terminal. Tell them it really exists—on the second level, with 30 lanes and kids bumper bowling. We actually have very fond memories of this place. In fact, it's something right out of *Funniest Home Videos*.

My son's Greenwich Village camp took a field trip here one summer afternoon. I decided to cut out of work during my lunch hour (I worked in midtown as a travel editor at a magazine) to surprise him and bowl for a bit. Alex was already bowling and thrilled to see that I had made it—as were the overwhelmed camp counselors who asked me to help out. When one of the young bowler's ball got stuck about half way down the lane (thanks to his gentle roll), I volunteered to retrieve it and proceeded to run down the lane. In a New York minute, I was completely up in the air and what seemed like slow motion landed prone. Who knew the lanes are slicked with oil? I heard the giggles and gasps before I even got up and I'll never forget my son's look as I walked back down the lane. It was the one time he wasn't clingy when I told him I had to go back to work. Tip: If the ball gets stuck, leave it.

HIKING

New York is about as flat as you can get, so don't expect much in the way of mountainous treks. Still, you can "hike" through parts of Central Park (see Central Park entry). We're guessing that you didn't come to New York in search of expert hiking. For that, you'll want to head to Westchester, Long Island, New Jersey or Connecticut.

GOLF & MINIATURE GOLF
Ferry Point Park Golf Course

Just south of the Whitestone Bridge in the Bronx (phone number not available at press time).

This 220-acre Jack Nicklaus-designed golf course is the first golf course to be built in the city in 35 years (an opening date of spring, 2005 is slated). The golf course will have a great waterfront location, a driving range and is only 20 minutes from midtown Manhattan. It operates on a daily-fee basis and is open to the public.

Clearview Park Golf Course

202-12 Willets Pt. Blvd. (Clearview Expressway), Queens, 718/229-2570, www.americangolf.com.

One of the most popular public courses in the metro area, this 8-hole course also affords golfers views of the Long Island Sound.

Dyker Beach Golf Course

86th Street and Seventh Avenue, Brooklyn, 718/836-9722 www.americangolf.com.

A public, 18-hole golf course, with views of the Verrazzano Narrows Bridge.

Golf Club at the Chelsea Piers

Pier 59 at Chelsea Piers, 23rd Street and the West Side Highway (at the Hudson River), 212/336-6400, www.chelseapiers.com.

A four-level, driving range that accommodates 52 golfers at one time. Bonus: Stunning Hudson River views (great sunsets) and heated stalls for year-round play. Works like a baseball hitting range: a computerized system in the floor spits a new ball up onto your tee immediately after you've smacked the previous one. The complex also houses a 1,000-square-foot practice putting green. Need lessons? Pros are available at the adjacent Jim McLean Golf Academy.

Randall's Island Family Golf Center

Randall's Island (drive across the Triborough Bridge or take the shuttle bus from 86th Street and Third Avenue), 212/427-5689.

Sports are what this no-frills, non-manicured park under the auspices of the Triborough Bridge are all about. My son will sometimes play double headers here with his baseball team on Sundays. You'll also find lively cricket matches, soccer games and flag football. Sometimes, a big event like a concert or, recently, the Cirque du Soleil, will take place on this Island. But for the most part, it's where kids and adults play team sports.

Pier 25 Mini-Golf

N. Moore Street (at West Side Highway), 212/732-7467.

Families travel way downtown—on bike or roller blades along the Hudson River bike path—to mini-golf at this 18-hole course. Don't expect windmills and other whimsical décor, this is no-frills mini golf.

HORSEBACK RIDING
Claremont Riding Academy

175 West 89th Street (between Columbus and Amsterdam avenues). 212/724-5100, www.potomachorse.com.

Close to Central Park, experienced riders *giddyap* along the bridle trail which loops around the Jacqueline Kennedy Onassis Reservoir (cost: about $50 an hour). There are also classes offered for kids ages 6 years old and up.

ICE SKATING/ROLLER SKATING
The Rink at Rockefeller Center

Fifth Avenue (49th and 50th), 212/332-7654, www.therinkatrockcenter.com

The queen of all ice skating rinks, to lace up and skate here is a quintessential New York City experience. Bonus: Skate during Christmastime when the lighted tree towers over the rink and your hearts will sing. Caveat: The rink is small and the holiday season is the busiest time in the city so plan it right—come when it first opens—or, be prepared to wait a long time in outdoor lines and to share the ice with the crowds. A nice touch: The rink is usually lined with tourists who enjoy the amateur show. The *Today Show* studios and plaza is a snowball throw away. In summer, the rink doesn't transform into a roller-skating rink like many other rinks. Instead, it becomes a lovely outdoor restaurant. For a short time in spring, a tent is draped over it and it becomes the scene for a spectacular orchid display. For information about admission and hours, call or visit the website.

Wollman Rink

Enter north of the Park entrance at 59th Street and 6th Avenue, 212/439-6900.

This outdoor ice skating rink has several things going for it. It's in Central Park with a midtown location, it affords skaters with great skyline views (at night is especially dramatic when it's all aglow) and it's teen heaven—rock music is piped in. There are restrooms and a casual snack bar for the requisite hot cocoa. Bonus: In the summer, Victorian Gardens at Wollman Rink Amusement Park takes over. For information about admission and hours, call or visit the website.

Sky Rink and the Roller Rinks at Chelsea Piers

Pier 61 at Chelsea Piers, 23rd Street, 212/336-6100, www.chelseapiers.com. Admission and hours: Call or visit the website for more information.

Challenge: Your Sarah Hughes-wannabe-daughter loves to ice skate but you'll be visiting New York in the middle of the summer. Enter Chelsea Piers, an ambitious sports complex with twin, year-round, indoor skating rinks. General skating time sessions are usually held in the afternoons and some evenings; call of check for updated schedules. Bonus: Views of the boats slipping by on the Hudson River give you a sense of place.

Chelsea Piers is also the spot for roller skating lovers and skateboarders. The complex has two open-air roller-skating rinks that are open for leisure skating on Saturday afternoons (they're in high demand by teams) during the week.

SPECTATOR SPORTS
Brooklyn Cyclones

Keyspan Park, 1904 Surf Ave. (West 17th-19th Streets), Coney Island, Brooklyn, 718/449-TIXS, www.brooklyncyclones.com.

The Class-A Mets Minor League Baseball team slugs here at Keyspan Park with the Coney Island Ferris wheel a home run hit away. You can reach the Park by subway: Take the Q local, W, F, or N train. The last stop on those trains is the Stillwell Avenue/Coney Island station. Exit the station towards Stillwell and Surf Avenues; the Park is two blocks away.

New York Giants & New York Jets

Meadowlands Sports Complex, The Meadowlands, East Rutherford, 201/935-3900, www.meadowlands.com.

New York's two football teams, the New York Giants and New York Jets, play at this sprawling, $450 million sports complex. For information about the Giants, call 201/460-4370. For information about the Jets, call 201/560-8200. To get to The Meadowlands, you can take a bus (it's a 20-minute ride) from the Port Authority terminal; round-trip bus service for all events is offered. Advanced-purchased ticket is required; call 800/772-2222 for more information.

New York Knicks

Madison Square Garden, 2 Penn Plaza (7th Avenue between 31st and 33rd Streets), hotline 212/465-JUMP, tickets 212/465-MSGI, www.thegarden.com.

One of the hottest tickets in town is a Knicks' ticket (especially if they're having a good season). We got lucky and snagged tickets for my son's birthday a couple of years ago—but then again, the Knicks stunk that year and so tickets were easier to come by. My son has been lucky enough to go to several Knicks games because his good friend Sam's father is a season ticket holder. But I also managed to buy last minute tickets at Tticketmaster. Knicks games are a ton of fun and there are usually celebs sitting courtside (Spike Lee, Woody Allen)—no matter how their team is doing.

New York Liberty

Madison Square Garden, 2 Penn Plaza (7th Avenue between 31st and 33rd Streets), 212/564-WNBA, www.nyliberty.com.

Women's professional basketball team that puts on a good show and that you have a chance of getting tickets to one of their games.

New York MetroStars

Giants Stadium at the Meadowlands, East Rutherford, New Jersey, 201/935-3900, www.metrostars.com.

Calling all soccer moms and dads—and their soccer loving kids. This decent professional soccer team plays March to October.

New York Mets

Shea Stadium, 1223-01 Roosevelt Avenue (126th Street), Flushing, Queens, 718/507-TIXX.

See listing on page 113.

New York Rangers

Madison Square Garden, 2 Penn Plaza (7th Avenue between 31st and 33rd Streets), 212/465-4459. www.thegarden.com.

New York's professional ice hockey team play a ton of games here (mostly at night) during the season. Tickets to a Rangers game, however, can be as difficult to score as to a Knicks game.

New York Sharks

Msgr. Farrell High School field, 2900 Amboy Road (Park St.-Tysens Lane, Staten Island, and August Martin High School field, 156-10 Baisley Blvd. (157th St.), Jamaica, Queens, 646/552-5798, www.nysharksfootball.com. Professional Independent Women's Football League.

New York Yankees

Yankee Stadium, 161st Street (River Avenue), Bronx, 212/307-1212, es.com www.yankees.com.

See listing on pages 118-119.

Staten Island Yankees

Richmond County Bank Ballpark at St. George (adjacent to Staten Island Ferry Terminal), Staten Island, 718/720-9265, www.siyanks.com.

This New York Yankees minor league affiliate showcases Yankees prospects in a cool stadium that overlooks New York Harbor. You can get to the Ballpark by subway: Take the 4 or 5 subway to Bowling Green or the N or R to the Whitehall Station, then hop on the Staten Island ferry (it's free). Exit the ferry from the lower deck and the ballpark is to your right. Note: The ferry departs every 15 minutes on weekdays between 5 and 7 pm, and every 30 minutes on weekends between 11:30 am and 7:30 pm. For more information about the ferry (including the holiday schedule), call 718/815-BOAT.

US Open Tennis Championships

USTA National Tennis Center, Flushing Meadows-Corona Park, 866-OPEN-TIX, www.usopen.org.

Tennis lovers know that this Tennis Center is home to one of four Grand Slam professional tennis events. The Center is located across the way from Shea Stadium. In fact, to get to the Center from Manhattan by train, you'll take the take the #7 subway to the Shea Stadium/Willets Point Station. The Tennis Center is a quick walk down the ramp from the station.

THEATERS

New York is home to 22 Broadway theaters and more-than-you-can-count off-Broadway and off-off Broadway theaters. For an up-to-date listing of current Broadway shows and theater addresses, go to www.playbill.com. Here are some kids' theaters and theaters that show occasional children's productions:

The Theater at Madison Square Garden

Seventh Avenue (between 31st and 33rd Streets), 212/307-1000, com www.thegarden.com.

The Christmas Carol is staged here each holiday season, as is the Ringling Bros. and Barnum & Bailey Circus and concerts.

New Victory Theater for Kids and Families

209 West 42nd Street (between Broadway and 8th Avenues), 646/223-3020, www.newvictory.org.

The New Victory is all about theatre for kids and families. All kinds of performances are produced here, including dance, comedy, theater and puppetry. Bonus: The price is right: Orchestra and mezzanine seats are $30 and balcony seats are $10. There are also VicTeens (kids 13 to 18 years old) and Junior VicTeens (kids 11 years old to 13) performances. Even the concession stands here won't break your budget: items like pretzels, cookies and raisins run $1 to $3.

York Theater at Saint Peters in Citicorp Center

Citicorp Center, Lexington Avenue at 54th Street, 212/935-5824.

This small theater produces kid shows, as well as adult shows.

Parent Tip

If you're the parent of a baby under the age of one, you no doubt crave an "adult" outing where baby is unequivocally welcome to cry, poop, spit up and nurse—without glares from others. Enter **Reel Moms, Bring Your Baby to the Movies**, a brilliant concept where you can go to an adult flick with your baby. The concept is offered in cities across the country. In New York, two theaters participate: **Loews 34th Street** (at 312 West 34th Street; 212/244-8850) and **Loews Orpheum 7** (at 1538 Third Avenue; 212/876-2111.

The way it works: Every Tuesday the theater features a full-length, current film. Doors open about an hour earlier than the showing so parents and babies can socialize. The movie is monitored for sound so loud noises don't startle baby and the lights are dimmed, so baby isn't frightened in a completely dark theater. At each of these theaters, bathrooms are equipped with changing tables. Tickets go on sale the day of the show at the ticket office. Mom or dad pays regular admission and babies are free. For more information, visit www.enjoytheshow.com.

Loews IMAX Theatre at New York City

Sony Theatres at Lincoln Square, 1998 Broadway at 68th Street, 212/336-5000, www.bigmoviezone.com.

There are a gazillion movie theaters around town, some showing kids movies, others featuring low-budget flicks. This 75-foot-high and 97-foot-wide screen theatre is in a class of its' own. My son flipped for the *Michael Jordan: To the Max* film (especially the part when he tells how he was cut from his school team!). Films are scheduled on a rotating basis

There's a smaller, albeit not much smaller (everything being relative), IMAX theater at The Museum of Natural History. (see listing under Museums section).

The Screening Room

54 Varick Street, 212/334-2100.

A 131-seat movie theater that has showings of *Breakfast at Tiffany's* every Sunday for kids 12 years old and up (and their parents). Cost: Adults $9, children $6. There's a restaurant here, too.

TADA! Youth Theater

15 West 28th Street (between Broadway and Fifth Avenue), 212/252-1619, www.tadatheater.com. Tickets: General admission tickets are $18 adults, $8 kids five years old and under.

The MO here is "by kids for kids." Actors ages 8 to 17 stage musicals so exciting they've been invited to perform at the White House. Nice touch: Restless kids can sit in seats or on mats on the floor.

TELEVISION TAPINGS

There are lots of television shows taped in the Big Apple and many of these programs invite audiences for free.

Note: Some of these shows you'll need to reserve your free seats weeks or months ahead of time so plan accordingly. Sometimes, though, standby tickets are available on the day of taping. (If you're willing to pay, go to www.newyorkshow.com and they'll help you secure tickets.)

Also, keep in mind that not all shows allow kids at tapings. Here is a sampling of shows that allow kids.

IMX

11 Penn Plaza (7th Avenue between 31st and 32nd Streets), 212/324-3461.

This is a hot daily music show on the FUSE network your 14 year old no doubt knows about (you must be 14 to 26 years old to be part of the on-camera audience.) Arrive at the studio by 4:30pm weekdays to see the performances by groups like Blink 182. If you arrive late and can't get in, don't worry; the studio is street level and the fans that hang outside also become part of the show. Bonus: Meet and greet the bands when they come outside. IMX records live Monday through Friday between 6 and 7 pm.

Late Night with Conan O'Brien

NBC Studios, 30 Rockefeller Plaza, 50th Street at Sixth Avenue, 212/664-3056, www.nbc.com.

Late Night With Conan O'Brien tapes Tuesday through Friday at 5:30 pm. Ticket reservations are accepted in advance only by calling the NBC ticket office at the above number. Advance reservations are limited to four tickets per group. Standby tickets are distributed on a first-come, first-serve basis at 9 am on the morning of the taping under the "NBC Studio" marquee at the 49th Street entrance to 30 Rockefeller Plaza. Stand-by tickets are limited to one per person and do not guarantee admission.

Last Call with Carson Daly

NBC Studios, 30 Rockefeller Plaza, 50th Street at Sixth Avenue, 212/664-3056, www.nbc.com.

To hear upcoming guests and to obtain tickets, call the number above. The show is taped live in NBC's Studio 8H in Rockefeller Center. Note: Kids must be 16 years old or older. You can reserve up to four tickets. Stand-by tickets are distributed on a first-come, first-serve basis at 11 am on the morning of the taping, under the "NBC Studios" marquee at the 49th Street entrance to 30 Rockefeller Plaza. One standby ticket is allotted per person and standby tickets do not guarantee admission.

The Daily Show with Jon Stewart

Daily Show Studios, 513 West 54th Street, 212/586-2477, www.daily show.com.

Kids under 18 aren't allowed to this Comedy Central show, but perhaps you can trade off with your spouse. Stewart and his sidekicks are hilarious. This is my favorite show on television—and my son's, too (yes, he is young but in my opinion the show is, if not totally appropriate at all times, generally speaking fine for teens to watch.) Our feeling is, my son wants to be informed about world events yet the newspaper and television accounts often include gory, graphic pictures that are far more disturbing than Stewart's comic take. The show tapes every Monday through Thursday at 5:45 pm. To request free audience tickets to attend a live taping, call the number above.

Live with Regis and Kelly

ABC Studios, West 66th Street between Columbus Avenue and Central Park West, 212/456-3054, www.tvplex.go.com/buenavista/livewithregis.

Caveat: There is a one year wait for snail mail tickets, but you can often snag same-day tix; arrive at the corner of 67th Street and Columbus Avenue around 7am to request a standby number. Standbys are seated if there are remaining seats after ticketholders have been seated. Children under 10 not admitted.

To order tickets in advance by mail, send a postcard to: *Live Tickets, Ansonia Station, P.O. Box 230777, New York, NY 10023-0777.*

Living It Up with Ali and Jack

CBS Broadcast Center, 524 West 57th Street, www.livingituptickets.com

Living It Up with Ali and Jack tapes live every Monday through Thursday, 9am to 10am; a second show tapes on Thursdays at 1pm. For tickets, write to: *Living It Up with Ali and Jack Audience Department,* CBS Broadcast Center, 524 West 57th Street, New York, NY 10019-2985. Include your name, address, phone number and email address. Children under 12 not admitted.

Saturday Night Live

30 Rockefeller Plaza, 50th Street (at 6th Avenue), 212/664-3056. www.*nbc.com.*

"Live from New York, it's Saturday Night Live." This is a tough ticket to snag thanks to its popularity. At press time, SNL said it would no longer take ticket requests until the summer of 2005. However, standby tickets are available: arrive no later than 7 am on the morning of the taping under the "NBC Studios" marquee (the 50th street side of 30 Rockefeller Plaza). You can choose standby tickets for either the 8pm dress rehearsal or 11:30 pm live show. One ticket allotted per person. Note: Standby tickets do not guarantee admission. Children under 16 years old not admitted to tapings.

The View

ABC Studios, 320 West 66th Street, www.abc.abcnews.go.com/theview/main.html.

To get free tickets in advance, send a postcard to: Tickets, *The View,* 320 West 66th Street, New York, NY 10023. Include your name, address and daytime phone number. Or, you can get tickets at *The View's* website by clicking on request show tickets. *The View* airs live Monday to Friday from 11 am to noon; arrival time is 9:30 am.

There is also a handful of live television shows with sidewalk studios that you don't need tickets for. Here's a sampling:

The Early Show

Fifth Avenue at 59th Street, www.cbsnews.com.

Housed in the General Motors Building at Trump International Plaza, you can watch the morning news show action on this ground level set through huge glass windows. Tapings are 7am to 9pm.

Good Morning America

Times Square (44th Street and Broadway), www.abcnews.go.com. Wake up with Diane Sawyer and Charles Gibson as they host this morning news show. The show airs every weekday from 7am to 9am. You can go inside the studio; for tickets fill out the form at the Website.

The Today Show

30 Rockefeller Plaza, Fifth to Sixth Avenues, www.nbc.com. *The Today Show* started the trend of sidewalk studios a couple of years ago. Sneak peeks at Katie Couric and Matt Lauer while they do this morning news show inside the studio on the ground floor at the corner of 49th Street and Rockefeller Center. The cameras often pan the crowd—to better your chances of being seen stand on the southeast corner—behind the anchor desk. *The Today Show* airs on weekdays between 7 am and 10am.

MOVIE SHOOTS

New York is extremely photogenic and has been the setting for many Hollywood blockbuster films and popular television shows. To get an up-to-date listing of movies or television shows currently being shot in the Big Apple, visit the Mayor's Office of Film, Theatre and Broadcasting's website at www.nyc.gov/film or call 212/307-6237.

PERFORMING ARTS
Carnegie Hall

154 West 57th Street (7th Avenue), 212/247-7800, www.carnegiehall.org. Ask a New Yorker on the street how to get to Carnegie Hall and they'll tell you to take the N, Q or R trains... ask my son and he'd say "practice, practice, practice." Alex has performed two piano solos here (in a recital with other children). Of course, Carnegie is also the stage for celebrated artists from all over the world. Alex's piano teacher is one of them—the famous pianist, Dr. Maria Botazzi. There are also fabulous kids' programs, including:

Saturday-afternoon Family Concerts, for kids age 5 to 10 years old. Cost: $5, including pre-concert activities and a child-friendly concert. Each child gets a copy of *KidsNotes,* an age-appropriate performance program. Bonus: After some of these concerts, a free screening of kids TV programs that relate to the event is presented at the Museum of Television & Radio following the concert.

CarnegieKids, for kids ages 3 to 6 years old, is held each spring and fall. Pre-schoolers get jazzed with these 45-minute concerts that are a mix of music and storytelling and motivate kids to get up and sing and dance. Cost: $3. Advance reservations are recommended.

Lincoln Center for the Performing Arts

Columbus Avenue between 62nd and 66th streets, 212/875-5350, www.lincolncenter.com.

This sprawling complex is home to several of the City's most important theaters. They are The Metropolitan Opera House, Avery Fisher Hall, Alice Tully Hall and NY State Theater. Everything from opera to dance to the symphony is performed here. Bonus: A tree at Christmas is decorated a la performing arts with trumpets and other musical instruments.

Also at Lincoln Center is the **New York City Ballet,** formerly the American Ballet Theater. When Mikhail Barishnikov danced with ABT I'd buy partial-view seats (cheap tix) and see every performance he danced. Then, I'd wait outside the stage door to catch a glimpse of him which, sadly, I never did. Misha no longer dances with the company but the New York City Ballet still puts on fabulous productions nonetheless, including *Swan Lake* and *Don Quixote.*

Celebrated trumpet player **Wynton Marsalis** hosts a series of family concert series such as "What is Jazz Piano" and "What is the Blues?" Costs are about $20 for adults and $15 for students. You can reserve them at the Alice Tully Hall box office on 65th Street or by calling CenterCharge, 212/721-6500.

Parent Tip

Jazz at Lincoln Center moves into its new home at the AOL Time Warner Center at Columbus Circle in Fall 2004 to become the world's first performing arts facility devoted to jazz. The impressive center will be perched high above Central Park, with bandstands posed against towering walls of glass. Called the Frederick P. Rose Hall, the facility will feature two theaters, a jazz club, a recording studio, several classrooms and the Ertegun Jazz Hall of Fame. The Hall of Fame will be a multi-media installation with interactive kiosks, projection screens and audio components. Bonus: Admission is free to all visitors of the hall.

BAM (Brooklyn Academy of Music)

30 Lafayette Street (between Ashland Place & St. Felix Street,) 718/636-4100, www.bam.org.

BAM is not about Emeril. BAM is home to contemporary and unique opera, dance, music, theatre, film and new media. There are several theatres here: the Howard Gilman Opera House, the Harvey Theater and BAM Rose Cinemas. BAM has tons of kid stuff throughout the year, including events like a special Father's Day concert with Tom Chapin and friends.

The Amato Opera Theatre

319 Bowery (close to 2nd Street), 212/228-8200, www.amato.org. Kid-friendly (shorter than the standard) operas are staged here in this intimate theater. Think: *Hansel and Gretel*, and you get the idea.

The Joyce

175 Eighth Avenue (at 19th Street), 212/242-0800, www.joyce.org. An intimate theater for fabulous avant-garde and modern dance performances.

Alvin Ailey American Dance Theater

55th Street and 9th Avenue, 212/767-0590, www.alvinailey.org. The largest facility devoted exclusively to dance in the country, set to open in the fall of 2004, with a 300-seat theatre, as well as 12 dance studios for the Alvin Ailey Dance Company.

Tribeca Performing Arts Center

199 Chambers Street, 212/220-1460, www.tribecapac.org. Family Folk & Fairytales, a downtown family performing arts series of classic children's tales set to music, with puppetry and acrobatics. Kids ages 3 to 10 years old. Tickets run between $8 and $13.

Parent Tip

If you are in town during the summer months, you won't want to miss one of the city's most delicious cultural pleasures—free performances in the parks. Here's a sampling of some of the best of them.

The New York Philharmonic, www.newyorkphilharmonic.org, 212/875-5000;

The Metropolitan Opera, www.metopera.org, 212/879-5900;

The Public Theater's Shakespeare in the Park, www.publictheater.org, 212/539-8500.

For info about some of the other free outdoor performances visit the Central Park Conservancy at www.centralparknyc.org or call the New York Parks and Recreation Hotline, 888/NYPARKS.

Getting Tickets

For Madison Square Garden events and big theatre productions:
- Ticketmaster, 800/755-4000, www.ticketmaster.com
- TeleCharge, 800/432-7250, www.telecharge.com
- Madison Square Garden, 212/465-MSG1, www.thegarden.com

For same-day tickets for off-Broadway and Broadway shows head to the TKTS booth, run by the Theatre Development Fund (212/221-0885, www.tdf.org). There are two TKTS locations. In midtown, there is a TKTS booth at Duffy Square (47th Street and Broadway). Hours: Monday through Saturday 3pm to 8pm for evening performances; Wednesday and Saturday 10am to 2pm for matinees; and Sunday 1 am to 8pm for matinees and evening performances.

Downtown, there is a TKTS booth at South Street Seaport at John and Front Streets (the rear of the Resnick/Prudential Building at 199 Water Street). Hours: Monday through Saturday 11am to 6 pm; Sunday 11am to 3:30pm. Many of the tickets are sold at half price, others are discounted at 25% (keep in mind that half price sounds great, but full ticket prices are sky high so it'll still cost you.) Note: You must pay in cash or with traveler's checks; credit cards are not accepted. And, there's a $2.50 service charge tacked on. The lines at

Parent Tip

Here are a few promotions you might wish to consider:

Each winter, New York offers **Paint the Town**, a promotion with American Express that features tremendous one, two, or four-night packages that include over 350 hotels, restaurants and activities and amenities—at affordable prices. Wintertime in New York is special, especially during the holidays when everything is gussied up in lights and decorations. Bonus: Visit the City when the snow is falling and the scene is magical. The Paint the Town promotion usually runs from the beginning of December through March. For more information, call 800/NYC-GUIDE, go to www.nycvisit.com or stop by the NYC's Official Visitor Information Center or one of the Visitor Information kiosks.

Each summer, New York offers **NYC Summer Breaks**, a summer promotion in conjunction with American Express. If visitors use their American Express card, they can benefit from tremendous savings on hotels, shows, restaurants, attractions and tours. To receive a copy of the NYC Summer Breaks call 800/NYC-GUIDE, go to www.nycvisit.com or stop by the NYC's Official Visitor Information Center or one of the Visitor Information kiosks.

Each year the League of American Theatres & Producers stages a one-night event called **Kids Night on Broadway**. Kids ages 6 to 18 years old get a free ticket to a Broadway show when accompanied by a paying adult. The promotion also includes restaurant and parking discounts and a special early curtain time. For more information, call 888/BROADWAY or visit www.kidsnightonbroadway.com.

❧

the TKTS booths can be extremely long (hours)—certainly not for youngsters. The uptown booth is centrally located in the thick of the Times Square action and kids will be preoccupied with the big city lights, as well as the street performers and taxis whizzing by (you're on an island in the middle of Broadway). Or, have one parent take the kids to the nearby Toy's 'R Us Ferris wheel or ESPN Zone while the other parent buys the tickets.

You can also get tickets by visiting the box office window of the show you'd like to see. Bonus: The box offices don't charge service fees. Even if a show is sold-out, arrive at the box office early in the day to inquire about rush tickets—last minute or returned or unsold seats. You might even end up with box seats!

You can also pick up discount coupons for many shows at NYC's Official Visitor Information Center, 810 Seventh Avenue at 53rd Street, 212/484-1222. Hours: Monday to Friday 8:30 am to 6pm, Saturday and Sunday 9am to 5pm.

Another option but it'll cost you: Ask your hotel concierge if they can help you secure theater tickets. Many concierges can spin magic; remember to tip.

Before you arrive in town, there are a number of ways you can get tickets to shows.

Go to the NYC & Company's website, www.nycvisit.com, and check out the Special Offers section and the Broadway News page. Also visit the Visitor Section, click on "Services" in the left-hand column and choose "Ticket Services." Bonus: If you sign up for the site's Visitor page you'll receive a monthly e-mail newsletter called "NYC This is Your City," filled with information about discounts on theater, hotels and attractions.

Resources
Miscellaneous
The Broadway Line: www.livebroadway.com.

The Theatre Direct International: www.broadway.com

Applause Theater & Entertainment Ticket Service: www.applause-tickets.com

TheaterMania: www.theatermania.com

Alliance of Resident Theatres: www.offbroadwayonline.com

Communications for the Parks Department (Special Events): 888/NY-PARKS

Moviefone 212/777-FILM

Lincoln Center Events 212/LINCOLN

Publications
Once you're in the Big Apple, there are excellent publications you should get your hands on that can be helpful to you while visiting. Some are distributed to hotel rooms. They include the following:

Time Out New York

Time Out New York Kids
WHERE Magazine
City Guide Magazine
IN New York Magazine
The Big Apple Parent
The Village Voice
New Yorker
New York Magazine
New York Observer

The New York Times weekend section (published on Friday) is full of happenings in the City's museums, theatres and attractions. Also, on Mondays, check out the Metro section's Cultural Happenings sidebar with listings about events that are scheduled to take place in the town during the upcoming week.

Budget Tips

Several of the museums and attractions in Manhattan have a "pay what you wish" policy in effect all the time (although they suggest admission prices), while others offer the policy during designated evenings. Here is a sampling of museums with a **"pay what you wish"** policy and the days/times this rule applies. (Note: For more detailed information about these museums and attractions, check out the listings in the appropriate chapters).

- **The Metropolitan Museum of Art** and **The Cloisters** (www.metmuseum.org, 212/535-7710). The suggested admission is $12 for adults, $7 seniors and children. However, what most people don't realize is that a "pay what you wish" policy is in effect *every* day.
- **The American Museum of Natural History** (www.amnh.org, 212/769-5100). The suggested admission is $12 adults, $9 seniors and students, $7 kids (two to 12 years old). However, every day is "pay what you wish."
- **The Museum of the City of New York** (www.mcny.org, 212/534-1672). The *suggested* admission is $12 for families, $7 adults, $4 seniors, students and children.
- **The National Museum of the American Indian** (www.nmai.si.edu, 212/514-3700). Admission is free.
- **The Museum of Modern Art** (www.moma.org, 212/708-9400) Pay-what-you-wish admission is Fridays from 4pm to 7:45pm.
- **Whitney Museum of American Art** (www.whitney.org, 800/WHITNEY) Pay-what-you-wish admission is Fridays from 6pm to 9pm.
- **Jewish Museum** (www.thejewishmuseum.org, 212/423-3200) Pay-what-you-wish admission is Thursdays from 5pm to 8pm.
- **Solomon R. Guggenheim Museum** (www.guggenheim.org, 212/423-3500) Pay-what-you-wish admission is Fridays from 6pm to 8pm.

- **Forbes Magazine Galleries** (www.forbesgalleries.com, 212/206-5548) Admission is free.
- **Brooklyn Children's Museum** (718/735-4400) It's free the first Thursday of each month or if you come Saturday or Sunday before noon.
- **The New York Hall of Science** offers free hours of admission that vary considerably throughout the year. (For specific dates and hours, visit www.nyhallsci.org, 718/699-0005).
- **The Bronx Zoo** has a pay-what-you-wish admission policy on Wednesdays.
- **The Staten Island Zoo** has a pay-what-you-wish admission policy on Wednesdays after 2pm.

Chapter 4

BASIC INFORMATION

Hospitals

People come from all over the globe to be treated at New York's hospitals.
• Columbia-Presbyterian Medical Center, 168th Street and Broadway, 212/305-2500
• Mount Sinai Medical Center, 98th Street and 5th Avenue, 212/241-6500
• New York Hospital/Cornell Medical Center, 70's and York, 212/746-5454
• New York University Medical Center, 34th Street and 1st Avenue, 212/263-5857
• Memorial Sloan-Kettering Cancer Center, 68th Street and York Avenue, 212/639-6835
• St. Vincent's Medical Center, 11th Street between 6th and 7th Avenues, 212/604-7000
• St. Lukes-Roosevelt Hospital, 115th Street and Amsterdam, 212/523-4000

All-Night Pharmacy

Call 800/748-3243 for listings of 24-hour pharmacies in the City.

Police

The number for police headquarters is 646/610-5000. In the event of an emergency, call 911.

Safety & Security

Ironically, since the September 11 terrorists attacks, New York City recently ranked 211 for crime out of 230 cities with populations over 100,000, also ranking the least amount of crime for the top 10 largest cities. That's remarkable. Still, you should be aware of your surroundings and be street savvy.

Some tips: Avoid desolate streets at night. Avoid Central Park at night. Don't carry a purse that does not have a zipper and carry it close to your body. I would also not recommend backpacks to carry infants and young babies; instead, carry your infant in front of you so you can see him or her at all times. Never leave your child in an unattended stroller—anywhere. Not only is it dangerous, it's illegal to do so. If you have older teens and are okay about giving them some space, buy a couple of walkie-talkies or, at the very least, a cell phone so you can be in contact with them.

In efforts to deter terrorism from striking New York City, you'll see heavy police presence at strategic locations including Grand Central Station, Penn Station and the Statue of Liberty. You can also be certain of tons of behind-the-scenes security and police, including radiation detectors, and bombproof garbage cans.

Security is beefed up, of course, at the New York City airports. You should anticipate waits at check-in, so arrive at the airport early.

Note that many New York City attractions do not allow you to enter with backpacks or packages, including Yankee Stadium, Shea Stadium, Madison Square Garden.

Visitor's Information & Help

There are several NYC & Company kiosks around town. They are:
New York City's Official Visitor Information Center
810 Seventh Avenue, between 52nd and 53rd Streets, 212/484-1222. Hours: Monday to Friday 8:30am to 6pm; Saturday, Sunday and holidays 9am to 5pm; Thanksgiving, Christmas and New Year's 9am to 3pm. Subway: Take the B, D, E to Seventh Avenue (and 53rd Street); N, R, S, Q to 57th Street; or 1,9 to 50th Street.

This is the city's official visitor's center where you can pick up free brochures and discount coupons to attractions and theater. There's also a MetroCard vending machine, an ATM machine and multilingual visitor information counselors.

City Hall Park Visitor Information
Located at the southern tip of City Hall Park on the Broadway sidewalk at Park Row. Hours: 9am to 6pm, Monday through Friday and 10am to 6pm Saturday and Sunday. Subway: The 1 and 2 to Park Place; the N, R, 4, 5 or 6 to Brooklyn Bridge/City Hall; the A, C to Broadway/Nassau Street; the E to WTC/Chambers; or the J, M, Z to Fulton Street.

Operating as the visitor gateway to Lower Manhattan, the kiosk features a multilingual staff who can give visitors directions, attraction brochures, event listings, maps and more.

Harlem Visitor Information Kiosk
Located at Adam Clayton Powell State Office Building plaza, 163 West 125th Street, east of Adam Clayton Powell Jr. Boulevard (Seventh Avenue). Hours: Monday through Friday 9am to 6pm, Saturday and Sunday 10am to 6pm. Subway: A, B, C, D, or 2,3 to 125th Street.

One of the newest kiosks, the fact that there is now an information center in Harlem now speaks volumes about the neighborhood as a tourist attraction.

Other places to get tourist information:
Federal Hall National Memorial
Located at 26 Wall Street. At press time a visitor information center was said to open here at a later date.

The Alliance for Downtown New York
120 Broadway, Ste. 3340 (between Pine and Cedar streets), 212/566-6700, www.downtownny.com. Open: Daily 10 am to 8 pm.

Brochures and guides and maps are yours for the asking here. You can also get tons of info on the website.

Brooklyn Tourism & Visitors Center
Brooklyn Borough Hall, 209 Joralemon Street (between Adam and Court streets), Brooklyn, 718/802-3846, www.brooklyn-usa.org. Open: Monday through Friday 10 am to 6 pm, Saturday 10 am to 5 pm

Information, brochures and maps about Brooklyn.

Grand Central I Love NY Booth
Grand Central Terminal main concourse, East 42nd Street (at Park Avenue), 212/340-2210, www.grandcentralterminal.com.

Visit the centrally located info booth with questions or take a free tour.

Times Square Alliance
1560 Broadway (between West 46th and West 47th streets), 212/869-1890, www.timessquarealliance.org. Open: Daily 8 am to 8 pm.

One-stop shopping for Metro Cards, maps, tours, you can even surf the Web.

Wall Street Rising Downtown Info Center
25 Broad Street (at Exchange Place), 212/425-4636. Open: Daily Monday through Friday 8:30 am to 7 pm, Saturday and Sunday 10 am to 4 pm.

Information center for lower Manhattan.

Chapter 5

READING LIST

Enrich your children's visit to New York City by encouraging them to read about the Big Apple—before they arrive or during their trip. New York plays a central role in many children's fiction books, and there are also non-fiction books that can be informative.

A friend of mine, Camille Purcell, is a respected librarian and mother of an elementary-school daughter Miranda and pre-school son Henry. Here are Camille's recommendations for great New York City reads.

Fiction
Miffy Loves New York City, Dick Bruna, Big Tent Entertainment (Ages 4 to 8)

The Adventures of Taxi Dog, Debra Barracca, Sal Barracca and Mark Buehner, Puffin, New York (Ages 4 to 9)

Uptown, Bryan Collier, Henry Holt and Company (Ages 4 to 8)

Milly and the Macy's Parade, Shana Corey, Scholastic Press, New York City (Ages 6 to 8)

Central Park Serenade, Laura Godwin, Joanna Cotler (Ages 4 to 8)

Snow White in New York, Fiona French, Oxford University Press (Ages 6 to 8)

My New York, Kathy Jakobesen, Little Brown and Company (Ages 5 and up)

Next Stop Grand Central, Maira Kalman, Putnam Pub Group, New York (Ages 4 to 8)

From the Mixed-Up Files of Mrs. Basil E. Frankweiler, E.L. Konigsburg, Simon Pulse (Ages 9 and up)

Micawber, John Lithgow, Simon and Schuster, New York (Ages 5 to 8)

The Old Pirate of Central Park, Robert Priest, Houghton Mifflin Company, New York (Ages 4 to 8)

This is New York, Miroslav Sasek, Universe Books (Ages 6 and up)

Hey Kid, Want to Buy a Bridge?, Jon Scieszka, Viking, New York (Ages 8 and up)

The Cricket in Times Square, George Selden, Random House, New York (Ages 9 and up)

Eloise, Kay Thompson, Simon and Schuster, New York (Ages 6 and up)

House on East 88ᵗʰ Street, Bernard Waber, Houghton Mifflin Company, New York (Ages 5 to 8)

Lyle, Lyle Crocodile, Bernard Waber, Houghton Mifflin Company, New York (Ages 5 to 8)

You Can't Take a Balloon into the Metropolitan Museum of Art, Jacqueline Preiss Weitzman, Dial Books for Young Readers, New York (Ages 4 and up)

Journey Around New York from A to Z, Marth and Heather Zschock, Commonwealth Editions, Massachusetts (Ages 4 to 8)

Non-Fiction
Brooklyn Bridge, Lynn Curlee, Atheneum Books for Young Readers, New York (Ages 8 and up)

Liberty, Lynn Curlee, Atheneum Books for Young Readers, New York (Ages 8 and up)

The Man Who Walked Between the Towers, Mordicai Gerstein, Millbrook Press (Ages 5 and up)

Under New York, Linda Oatman High, Holiday House, New York (Ages 5 and up)

Empire State Building, Elizabeth Mann, Mikaya Press, New York (Ages 9 and up)

The Brooklyn Bridge, Elizabeth Mann, Mikaya Press, New York (Ages 9 and up)

Storied City: A Children's Guide to New York City, Leonard S. Marcus, Dutton, New York (All ages)

The Inside-Outside Book of New York City, Roxie Munro, Dodd, Mead and Company, New York (Ages 5 and up)

Chapter 6

WHERE ARE WE GOING NOW?

Young Kids' Itinerary
Day One
Morning

Enjoy breakfast at one of the city's diners.

If kids are old enough (see information under Lower Manhattan chapter), head way downtown to Lower Manhattan to visit St. Paul's Chapel and Ground Zero. Then, take the ferry and visit Ellis Island and the Statue of Liberty. Note: You can also opt to visit just Ellis Island or just the Statue of Liberty (the ferry stops first at the Statue and then onto Ellis). A round-trip ferry ticket to Ellis Island and Statue of Liberty is $8 for seniors. You can buy advanced tickets by calling 800/600-1600. (For more information, see info under Ellis Island and Statue of Liberty entry.)

If you're not up for visiting the Statue of Liberty or Ellis Island but would like to see the Statue, board the Staten Island ferry for a ride that will afford great views of Lady Liberty. The best part: the ferry is free roundtrip.

Afternoon

If you do visit Ellis Island or the Statue of Liberty, you can purchase lunch at either spot (or, pick up sandwiches in town to bring with you). Otherwise, when you disembark the ferry in lower Manhattan, make your way up to Soho and the Village and lunch at one of the restaurants we've listed in that section (Balthazar in Soho is a great spot). After lunch, stroll the streets of Soho and the Village. Then, it's naptime/rest back at the hotel. Or, if your hotel has a pool, take a swim.

Evening
Have dinner at one of the family-friendly restaurants in Times Square (see listings). Or, if you dare, dine at a more upscale affair like the Oyster Bar in Grand Central Station.
Take in a Broadway show or an IMAX movie.

Day Two
Morning
Rise and shine and grab breakfast at a diner or bagel shop.
If it's a lovely day, go to the Central Park Zoo. If not, spend the morning at the American Museum of Natural History—or, if your children love art, opt for the Metropolitan Museum of Art, Museum of Modern Art, the Guggenheim Museum or the Whitney Museum of Art.

Afternoon
Lunch at one of the museums. Or, head to Central Park to dine at the Boathouse restaurant.
If you're up for it, rent a rowboat and take an easy row on the lake after lunch. Otherwise, stroll over to the Zoo (if you didn't hit it in the morning) or take a spin on the Carousel.
Take tea at the Plaza Hotel or the Waldorf Astoria.
Then, back to the hotel for rest and/or a swim.

Evening
Dinner at Tavern on the Green.
A visit to the top of the Empire State Building (closes at midnight).

Teenagers' Itinerary
Okay, first off, there's a huge difference between traveling with a teenage girl and a teenage boy. In a word: shopping. Your son could care less about shopping; your daughter could care less about anything else. And so, the following itineraries are skewed to please both genders.

Day One
Morning
Thanks to hormone overdrive, they'll want to sleep in. Remind them that they are in the City That Never Sleeps. Grab breakfast at a New York City diner. Then, take the subway to Brooklyn and walk across the Brooklyn Bridge to Manhattan (or, if you're up for it, take the subway to South Street Seaport, grab breakfast there, then walk across the Brooklyn Bridge *and back.*)

Visit St. Paul's Chapel and the World Trade Center site

Board ferry for Statue of Liberty/Ellis Island. Or, if you're not interested in visiting either but would like to see the Statue of Liberty, hop aboard the Staten Island ferry and take the free roundtrip ride that gives you a nice view of Lady Liberty.

Afternoon

If you've decided to go to Ellis Island, you can buy and eat lunch there. Otherwise, make your way up to the Lower East Side to stroll Orchard, Grand and Delancey streets—chock-full of bargain shops and a buzz of activity.

Chinatown is spot-on for dim sum lunch.

Tour the Lower East Side Tenement Museum on Orchard Street.

Evening

Dinner at family-friendly Times Square restaurant (see listing). After dinner, see *Stomp,* or *Blue Man Group,* off-Broadway shows that teens love.

If you've got the pizzazz, top off the evening at the city's only revolving rooftop restaurant and lounge, The View Restaurant and Lounge in the Marriott Marquis located in Times Square.

Day Two

Morning

They'll want to sleep in but tell them they can check their email at the easyInternet Café in Times Square while munching on bagels and that should help. If you're the lucky parent of a kid who could care less about the Internet, you have several options. If it's a nice day and your hotel is near Central Park or one of the City's other grassy spots, do like a New Yorker—grab a couple of bagels with cream cheese and the New York *Times* and enjoy a picnic breakfast. Or, opt to eat at one of the many diners around town or bagel shops.

Then, head for Times Square. Visit the Madame Tussaud Wax Museum. Later, stroll Times Square enjoying the street performers and neon scene. Teenage daughter tip: Stroll Fifth Avenue, window shopping along the way in the fabulous shops like Bendels, Tiffany & Co., Cartier, Saks Fifth Avenue and Cartier. On the other end of the cash flow spectrum, there's a gigantic H & M. Begin your outing at Rockefeller Center and St. Patrick's Cathedral across the street and walk uptown. You'll eventually come to 59th Street, flanked by the Plaza Hotel and FAO Schwarz, with Central Park a chestnut throw away. If your daughter insists on visiting Bloomingdales, walk east to Lexington Avenue. (You could visit the spanking new Bloomies in Soho later in the trip). Teenage son tip: He'll also enjoy strolling Fifth Avenue thanks to the incredible NBA Store and Niketown.

If your son or daughter is a jock or a sports fan, head to ESPN Zone for lunch. Let them loose in the games area before settling in for lunch at the restaurant. Or backpedal a couple of blocks to Ellen's Stardust Diner at 51st and Broadway.

Afternoon

Now that you've satiated—or at least whet their appetites—for the things *they* like to do it's time to hit a museum. The Museum of Natural History is a must. But the Met is also an incredibly rich experience.

Evening

If you're in town during baseball season, why not head to the ballpark for a game and dinner? You have two choices: Yankee Stadium or Shea Stadium. Both are accessible by subway of boat (see individual listings). Or, head uptown to Yankees Stadium just to take the really cool Stadium tour.

If you're in town when baseball isn't, get tickets to a Broadway show. Or, you might be able to get Knicks or Rangers tickets for games at Madison Square Garden.

For dinner, go to America (see listing).

After dinner (if you aren't at the ballpark or a Broadway Show) go to the top of the Empire State Building to see the City lights (open until midnight). Or, take the subway uptown to the roof sculpture garden at the Met Museum for pretty city views (seasonal).

Day Three

Morning

Okay, let them sleep in a little bit today and then go for a late breakfast at Balthazar in Soho.

Afternoon

Hit fashionable Soho. Peek into galleries and boutiques.

Stroll up to Greenwich Village to hang out.

For lunch, go to Little Italy for pizza or John's Pizza in the Village.

Next up: Teenage boys and girls who are sports enthusiasts will love Chelsea Piers, a gigantic sports complex (see listing). Take the Chelsea *Screamer* boat sightseeing tour around Manhattan (it leaves from Chelsea Piers).

Evening

Take the subway to Grand Central Station to check it out (rush hour is a good time to see all the action). Have dinner at the Oyster Bar in Grand Central or at Mickey Mantle's restaurant or back to Times Square where there are tons of family-friendly theme restaurants that kids love.

Check out the listings in the local papers, etc. for a concert, dance performance or theater performance.

Parent Tips

• Your teens will love to stay in touch with friends at the easyInternet Café, the world's largest Internet café. Located in Times Square, the café has 800 PC's.

• If you're in town on a Sunday afternoon, bring your teenager to Blue Smoke/Jazz Standard, a restaurant/club on East 27th between Park and Lexington. Between 1pm and 3pm the downstairs club features jazz by kids for kids. Talented New York City high school jazz musicians perform the jazz. The cover charge is $5, and you can order off a menu—or order nothing at all and just enjoy the music. Bonus: Kids of all ages are allowed in and there's a space for them to dance or burn off energy. Yes, parents are allowed in, too. Note: You'll need to make reservations: 212/576-2232.

My 13-year-old (Alex's) Picks

ESPN Zone
Broadway Show
Mickey Mantle Restaurant
The Chelsea Screamer boat ride
Yankees game at Yankee Stadium

Alex's 17-year-old sister's (Elizabeth's) Picks

Times Square for souvenirs like T-shirts
A deli sandwich from a New York Deli
A slice of New York pizza
A Broadway Show
Grand Central Station ("Be sure to look up at the constellation on the ceiling.")
Central Park

New York CityPass

We recommend that you purchase a New York CityPass, which gets you into six of the City's most celebrated attractions for one price. The attractions are: The American Museum of Natural History, the Empire State Building Observatory & NY Skyride, the Intrepid Sea Air Space Museum, the Guggenheim Museum, the Museum of Modern Art, and Circle Line Sightseeing Cruises. The booklet also entitles you to a discount on a dinner or brunch cruise on the World Yacht, as well as discounts to Bloomingdale's.

The way it works: Purchase your CityPass booklet at the first of these six attractions you visit (the booklet is sold at each one of them). Bonus: You also avoid most ticket lines. The City Pass booklet is valid for only nine days, beginning the first day you use it. For more information, go to www.citypass.com; you can also purchase tickets online at this website.

The New York Pass, a "passport" to New York that gives users free entry to more than 40 attractions, as well as unlimited subway and bus transportation, is another good money saver. This pass also allows visitors to bypass lines at some attractions. For more information and pricing, call 877-714-1999 or go to www.newyorkpass.com.

Traveling With Your Pets

One of your pet peeves might be that refuse to leave your family's beloved mutt at home. No need to whimper. New York is a pet-friendly town with hotels that will welcome your pet and dog runs in a number of parks Here are some hotel recommendations for a pet-friendly vacation:

The New York Dog Spa & Hotel
145 West 18th Street, 212/243-1199, www.nydogspa.com

Tribeca Grand Hotel
2 Avenue of the Americas, 877-519-6600, www.tribecagrand.com

Soho Grand Hotel
310 West Broadway, 800/965-3000, www.sohogrand.com

Hotel Gansevoort
18 Ninth Avenue (at 13th Street), 877-726-7386, www.hotelgansevoort.com

Courtyard by Marriott—Manhattan/Times Square South
114 West 40th Street, 800/228-9290, www.courtyardtimessquare.com

Hotel 41
206 West 41st Street, 212/703-8600, www.hotel41.com

Le Parker Meridien Hotel
118 West 57th Street, 800/543-4300, www.parkermeridien.com

Crown Plaza at United Nations
304 East 42nd Street, 212/986-8800, www.sixcontinentshotels.com

The Stanhope, A Park Hyatt Hotel
995 5th Avenue (at 81st Street), 212/774-1234, www.hyatt.com

LOWER MANHATTAN

Lower Manhattan is a heady mix of young stockbrokers in pinstripes (no, not the Yankees), seasoned politicians in partisan power suits and historic churches shadowed by soaring skyscrapers. This bustling part of the city, where the East and Hudson rivers meet, was also our nation's first capital. Unfortunately, this special part of Manhattan is now etched in most of the world's memory as the tragic spot where this country's most devastating act of terrorism hit on 9/11.

In addition to the financial center of the world—lower Manhattan is home to the New York Stock Exchange and Wall Street (originally a walled fortress built by Dutch setters in 1663)—it's also home to City Hall, where the city government is housed.

Strolling the streets in lower Manhattan is a humbling experience. On a recent weekend visit, we stumbled across a Nicolas Cage movie shoot that attracted lots of excitement. Visit here on a weekday and the action begins when the bell rings at the Stock Exchange. Yet, while it may seem as business as usual, since 9/11 there is a tremendous void down here—quite figuratively, literally and spiritually—that will never in a million years be filled.

If your children are old enough—or, rather, are mature enough (it really doesn't matter how old they are biologically as each child's capacity for handling emotions differs)—I recommend you begin your visit to New York City in lower Manhattan, specifically at St. Paul's Chapel and Ground Zero. It is a gentle reminder of the spirit and determination of this City, which you'll come to appreciate even more during your vacation here as you make your way uptown to explore all of the neighborhoods. Be prepared for your children to ask many questions and to relive their feelings and emotions on that day. If they were old enough at the time, they'll forever remember where they were on 9/11 and a visit to the World Trade Center site will most likely cause them to revisit those memories.

Like millions of Americans on the morning of 9/11, I dropped my son off at school and got on a train to go into the city to work. As my train approached Manhattan I saw the burning towers. Cell phones rang in the train car and word quickly spread among the commuters that the city was under attack. Some of my commuter friends had loved ones in the Towers. I also had friends who worked in the Towers. We watched in disbelief and confusion. I was separated from my son, ten years old at the time, and couldn't reach him because the phones were all out. Fighter jets flew over his school and they were not allowed outside at recess. He'd been told something had happened in Manhattan and he knew I was headed there to work that day.

My son doesn't want to visit the World Trade Center site. The day still haunts him. Your child may also not want to visit for similar reasons—or you, as their parent, may not want them to. It's a personal decision and one which parents should give some thought to beforehand.

Federal Hall National Memorial
26 Wall Street (at Broad St.), 212/825-6888, www.nps.gov/feha.
Open: Closed Saturday, Sunday.
Admission: Free.
Subway: 2, 3, 4. 5, J, M, and Z.

This is where George Washington was inaugurated back in 1789. You can take a guided tour (or a self-guided tour) to see the Bible that Washington used at his inauguration and there are also several interactive exhibits. There's also a junior ranger program during which kids learn about the American Revolution and George Washington.

St. Paul's Chapel

Broadway (between Fulton and Vesey Streets, adjacent to World Trade Center site), 212/233-4264, www.saintpaulschapel.org.

Open: The Ground Zero Ministry Exhibit is open Monday through Saturday from 10am to 6pm and Sunday from 9am to 4pm; a concert series takes place on Mondays between 1pm and 2pm (during which the exhibit closes). There is also a Prayers for Peace worship service held daily between 12:30pm and 12:45pm.

Admission: Free.

For years, this darling church with its pretty stained glass windows and pews has had a special spot in the hearts of New Yorkers—and the country. After all, it is Manhattan's oldest public building in continuous use (it was built in 1766) and was George Washington's post-inauguration place of worship. And then the World Trade Center Towers, located just next door, came tumbling down, destroying everything in its path—except miraculously St. Paul's, which instantly became home base for firefighters, police and other rescue teams. In order to appreciate the full story and the enormity of 9/11, you should visit St. Paul's "Unwavering Spirit" exhibit, which takes over the entire church with 23 artifacts from the nine-month period when St. Paul's was the makeshift site for volunteer relief efforts. Artifacts include poignant pictures of people who lost their lives that day, banners that were stitched with heartfelt thanks from people around the world to New York's bravest, audio and video tapes, and a cot where firefighters and policemen took respite. In fact, following the days immediately after 9/11, the church was lined with cots on which relief effort volunteers would place a stuffed animal for the firefighters and other rescue teams to take comfort.

You'll also notice the boxes of tissues that have been placed throughout the church, an appreciated gesture by the teary visitors to this extremely moving and tasteful 9/11 shrine.

National Museum of the American Indian

Smithsonian Institution.
The George Gustav Heye Center.
Alexander Hamilton U.S. Custom House.
One Bowling Green (across from Battery Park).
212/514-3700, www.americanindian.si.edu.

Subway: 4, 5 to Bowling Green, 1, 9 to South Ferry, N, R to Whitehall St. and M, J, Z to Broad Street.

Open: Daily 10am to 5pm. Open until 8pm on Thursday. Closed Christmas day.

Admission: Free.

The setting of this museum is one reason to visit—it's located in the historic U.S. Customs House building. Other reasons: live performances, films and rooms from a contemporary reservation (schoolroom, a family's living room) bring your kid's textbook pages to life. Bonus: Many of the guides are Native American.

World Trade Center Site

There is a viewing area at Liberty Street and Broadway.

Your first tip that you're near the site where the World Trade Center Towers once stood is the line of tour buses surrounding it. Your second clue will be the silence of the visitors who stroll and absorb the what-now-resembles a pit with construction equipment. The site is fenced in and you can walk all the way around it. There has been a lot of controversy surrounding what will be built here, if anything. Some New Yorkers want to see another skyscraper; others view it as a burial ground that should be immortalized as a meditation park. As this book went to press, the plans were not final.

Especially poignant is The Viewing Wall with the names of those who died, and 17 history panels that tell the story of the evolution of Manhattan from colonial times to today.

Winter Garden Atrium/World Financial Center

West Street (between Liberty and Vesey streets), 212/945-0505, www.worldfinancialcenter.com.

Subway: 1, 2, 3, 9, E, N, R.

Located in Battery City Park on the Hudson River, The World Financial Center houses four office towers (including American Express and Merrill Lynch). The office towers are connected by a string of courtyards, including the spectacular Winter Garden Atrium. Here, there are great restaurants to eat in (Japanese, Chinese, steak, seafood, coffee, juice bar) and shops to explore (Banana Republic, Godiva, Ann Taylor). If it's a lovely day, grab a sandwich or made-your-way salad at Cosi (there are several Cosi shops around Manhattan; the fresh-from-the-oven bread is fantastic) and go outside to sit in one of the public gardens here or along the Esplanade with river views.

Bonus: The Winter Garden Atrium is the stage for year-round performing arts festivals and performances. Check the website above for upcoming events.

Note: The World Financial Center and Winter Garden Atrium is a five-minute walk from Ground Zero. And, the Museum of Jewish Heritage also makes its home here.

The Skyscraper Museum

39 Battery Place.

212/968-1961, www.skyscraper.org.

Open: Wednesday through Sunday noon to 6pm.

Admission: General $5, students and seniors $2.50.

Subway: 4 or 5 to Bowling Green, R or W to Whitehall St. 1 or 9 to Rector St.

Located on the ground floor of the Ritz-Carlton Hotel on the southern tip of Battery Park City, this spanking new museum is a tribute to New York's architectural heritage and the individuals behind it. It includes VIVA, a 3-D Computer model of Manhattan.

South Street Seaport

Visitor's Center is located at 209 Water Street (Fulton Street), 212/SEA-PORT, www.southstseaport.com.

Subway: 2, 3, 4, 5, A, C, J, M, Z.

Open: Daily 10am to 6pm.; October through March open until 5pm.

Admission: Free to the marketplace; to the museum—$5 adults, free for kids' twelve years old and under.

A fantasy of upscale shops and eateries housed in a historic seaport and festive marketplace with ongoing live entertainment that's similar to Boston's Faneuil Hall and Quincy Market. There's also the South Street Seaport Museum here with buildings that include a tiny children's museum, printing shop and boat-building shop. The best part: The historic ships that kids can climb aboard or you can take a cruise on (see the *Pioneer* under boat sightseeing).

New York City Police Museum

100 Old Slip (four blocks south of South Street Seaport).

212/480-3100, www.nycpolicemuseum.org.

Subway: 4, 5 to Bowling Green, 1, 2 to Wall Street, N, R to Whitehall, South Ferry.

Open: Tuesday through Saturday 10am to 5pm.

Admission: (Suggested donation) Adults $5, seniors $3, kids (ages 6 to 18 years old) $2.

Parent Tip

The **Seaport** also houses an ambitious and inexpensive food court on the top level of the complex with giant windows that peer out onto the harbor. The eateries are easy on the wallet and, we don't need to tell you that kids love food courts.

☙

Way back when, the NYPD's 1st Precinct once called this museum home. Today, kids can learn about the history and the culture of New York's finest. There are permanent and rotating exhibits. Wall of Heroes is devoted to 9/11 and depicts the role that the New York Police Department played with on-camera interviews, photos and Ground Zero artifacts. In other exhibits, there's a Harley Davidson police motorcycle, shields, uniforms, a mugshot camera and a firearms training stimulator.

The Museum of Jewish Heritage—A Living Memorial to the Holocaust

18 First Place (at Battery Park), 646/437-4200, www.mjhnyc.org. Subway: 4, 5, W, R, 1, 9, J, M, Z.

Open: Sunday through Tuesday and on Thursday 10am to 5:45pm, Wednesday 10am to 8pm, Friday 10am to 5pm (daylight savings time), Friday eve of Jewish holidays 10am to 3pm. Closed Saturday, Jewish holidays and Thanksgiving.

Admission: $10 adults, $7 seniors, $5 students, kids 12 years old and under are free. Free admission every Wednesday from 4pm to 8pm.

A newly expanded museum that tells the story of Jews in the 21st century through a collection of personal objects, original films and other artifacts. The first and third floor house exhibits are child friendly. However, the second floor exhibit, *Ours to Fight For: American Jews in the Second World War* might be disturbing for young children and so the museum warns parents to visit the exhibit first before allowing their young kids to do the same. Nice touch: the Garden of Stones Memorial Garden in honor of Holocaust survivors and those who died.

Touring Lower Manhattan

Who says you have to have deep pockets on Wall Street? Take the *free*, 90-minute **walking tour**, stopping off at Wall Street and the New York Stock Exchange (since 9/11 the Stock Exchange has been closed to visitors). Tours run every Thursday and Saturday beginning at noon. Meet at the front steps of the National Museum of the American Indian. Reservations aren't necessary. For more information, call 212/484-1222 or visit www.nycvisit.com.

Or, opt to take the self-guided **Patriotic Trail** (a better bet for families with young kids because you can stop at your leisure). This tour will take you about an hour (without stopping.) It begins one block east of the World Trade Center site at Broadway and Vesey Street and takes you to 19 sites that figured prominently in the birth of the nation. Pick up a brochure at NYC & Company's information kiosk in City Hall Park, or download it from www.nycvisit.com/lowermanhattan.

෨

Children's workshops take place on Sundays and be sure to pick up the family guide (geared for children ages 7 to 11 years old), *"You Are A Museum Detective—The Case: Looking for Heritage in All the Right Places."*

Bonus: The museum is also home to Abigael's Café run by celebrated chef Jeff Nathan, host of the Kosher gourmet cooking show, "New Jewish Cuisine." The café serves hot entrees, wraps, salads and other items that are made according to Jewish dietary laws.

Parent Tips

• Head to the top floor deck of **Pier 17** which juts into the East River to recline in a deck chair and watch New York Harbor and the Brooklyn and Manhattan bridges.

• When you and the kids are pooped from too much pounding the pavement, jump on the **Downtown Connection**, a free bus service for visitors (as well as residents and workers). The route runs between South Street Seaport and northern Battery Park City. The best part: You can hop on and off the bus at designated stops.

• Sugar coat your downtown visit with a stop to **Candy World**, owned by Alan Silver for more than 30 years. Located at 88 Chambers Street, a lot of the sweet stuff is made right in the shop. The shop suffered considerable damage in the 9/11 attacks—the nut roasters, chocolate machines and ice cream makers were kaput. But Silver wasn't going to let the terrorists turn his business sour and he was back up in a month.

SOHO, NOHO, TRIBECA, GREENWICH VILLAGE, EAST VILLAGE & LOWER EAST SIDE

In a word: Cool. This funky, trendy part of town is always tops on the list of teens. Think: body piercing, blue and green hair, revealing clothing and a got-to-be-me vibe. This is the City's hipster spot. I've lived in both Soho and Greenwich Village and loved every minute.

When I lived in Soho right out of college, it was sleepy and very neighborhoody with wonderful galleries and unique shops that attracted visitors on spring, summer and fall weekends. Soho's had a major wake-up call (critics call it a rude awakening) but I still love it down here. It's certainly not as sleepy, but it's still appealing. Peanut Butter and Company is on Soho's Sullivan Street, one of the city's most popular kid-friendly eateries.

Lower East Side Tenement Museum

90 Orchard Street (at Broome Street), 212/431-0233, www.tenement.org.

Open: The main Gallery is open daily 11am to 5:30pm; afternoon tours run often Tuesday through Fridays and Saturday and Sunday beginning at 11am.

Admission: Free admission to Gallery. Tours: $9 adults, $7 students and seniors.

Manhattan's Lower East Side once served as a "Gateway to America," and this museum depicts those early days. Recreated tenement apartments that tell the tales of immigrants are set up to depict the cramped, impoverished living quarters that these immigrants experienced. To fully absorb the story, it's best to take one of the tours. The best: *The Confino Family Apartment,* based on the Sephardic-Jewish Confino family from Kastoria (once part of the Ottoman Empire, now in Greece.) An interpreter in full costume plays the part of teenager Victoria Confino in 1916. She welcomes museum visitors as though you had just arrived from your homeland and teaches you how to adapt to America. Lively and educational for all ages.

Note: The Confino program costs extra— $8 adults, $6 students and seniors. Keep in mind, any two programs/tours cost $14 adults, $10 students and seniors; any three programs/tours combination costs $20 adults, $14 students and seniors. The Confino program takes place on afternoon weekends; advance reservations or not required, but you can do so. Visit the website or call for exact times.

Parent Tips

• The **Scholastic Store** in Soho is a fun-loving kids-only bookstore that stocks not only educational toys and books, but also a 298-seat, giant screen theater too. Most of the shows are geared to the preschool set. Located at 557 Broadway (near Prince Street); call 212/343-6166.

• **Bloomingdale's** has made its home on the East Side for years, and now it's got a downtown sidekick; a sister store in Soho. The new Bloomies is much smaller than its uptown sibling and has a downtown, Soho edge to it. Located at 504 Broadway (between Spring and Broome Streets); 212/729-5900, www.bloomingdales.com.

Forbes Magazine Galleries

60 Fifth Avenue (at 12th Street), 212/206-5548, www.forbescollection.com.

Subway: F, L, N, Q, R.

Open: Tuesday, Wednesday, Friday and Saturday 10am to 4pm. Closed Sunday, Monday and Thursday and major holidays.

Admission: Free (No strollers).

There are two operative words for families thinking of visiting this museum: toys and free (no, not free toys!). You don't have to pay to enter this small gem of a museum that's a showcase for Forbes' collection of toy boats and soldiers, as well as a quirky collection of Faberge Easter eggs, Monopoly games, medals and trophies and Presidential papers (Forbes was a compulsive collector).

Children's Museum of the Arts

182 Lafayette Street (between Broome and Grand streets), 212/941-9198, www.cmany.org.

Subway: 6, N, R.

Open: Wednesday noon to 7pm, Thursday through Sunday noon to 5pm

Admission: $5; pay-what-you-wish on Wednesday 5pm to 7pm.

A sweet museum that's much smaller than the Upper West Side Children's Museum, this downtown spot has many programs and events for kids throughout the year (check the website or call for updates). Permanent attractions include a Creative Play Area (for kids 5 years and under); an Artists Studio (for kids five years and older) with daily art projects; an Actors Studio (for kids of all ages) with costumes and instruments; a Ball Pond (for kids of all ages), a cushioned space with large physio balls; and Magnetic Masterpieces with reproductions of famous artworks, cut into magnetic puzzle pieces that kids can arrange. The Upper West Side children's museum is more popular, but this low-key downtown museum doesn't tend to get super crowded.

Parent Tip

Buy the ultimate souvenir while visiting NoHo at **Bond No. 9 New York**. The shop sells custom fragrances named after New York City neighborhoods, from Park Avenue to the Lower East Side to Chelsea—or a combo of several of your favorite neighborhoods. Located at 9 Bond Street, 212/228-1940.

CHELSEA

There's not a whole lot of stuff going on for kids in this lively neighborhood except for Chelsea Piers, which kids and adults adore. Otherwise, it is fun to stroll through Chelsea to window shop and poke around in some of the galleries.

Chelsea Piers

West 23rd Street (at the Hudson River), 212/336-6666, www.chelseapiers.com.

Open: The operating schedule varies depending on the activity. Call or visit the website for specific information.

Admission: The cost depends on the activity. Call or visit the website for specific information.

Subway: C, E.

Sporty New York families practically live at this sprawling 30-acre sports and recreation complex with baseball hitting cages, ice-skating rinks (see entry under skating), basketball courts, a driving range (see entry under golf), indoor soccer fields, a rock-climbing wall and lots more.

Get this: Parents Night Out is offered on Saturday evenings between 7pm and 11pm. Cost: $40 for the first child, $20 each sibling. You must make reservations.

Parent Tip

A nice contrast to the Chelsea Pier Complex is the off-the-beaten-path **gardens** at the **General Theological Seminary of the Episcopal Church** on Ninth Avenue (between 20th and 21st streets). The Seminary property, which dates back to 1827 was donated by Clement Clark Moore, a professor at the Seminary and, of course, the alleged author of the famous poem which begins, "'Twas the night before Christmas." The 32,000-square-foot garden that's home to 60 trees, 35 flowerbeds and a handful of benches—a perfect respite from the busy streets of Manhattan. The gardens are open Monday through Friday between noon and 3pm and Saturday between 11am and 3pm, closed on Sunday.

THEATER DISTRICT/TIMES SQUARE

When I was growing up on Long Island, and my parents would surprise us with tickets to a Broadway show for our birthday or Christmas, I would jump up with joy and land with fear. I was afraid of Times Square, where most of the Broadway theaters are housed. I knew we'd be walking late at night down a desolate, drug-infested street to our car that would inevitably be parked in a distant parking garage. I dreaded the outing.

Times Square has morphed into a lively, safe family mecca, thanks to a total facelift and renovation project spearheaded by former Mayor Rudolph Guliani. There are tons of family activities in Times Square, as well as family-friendly restaurants and hotels. And, in fact, *USA Today* recently named Times Square one of the top 10 places in the United States to visit. That is just incredible considering ten years ago Times Square was a place recommended to stay *far away from* when visiting the City.

ESPN Zone

1472 Broadway, 212/921-ESPN, www.espnzone.com .

Open: Sunday 11am to 11pm, Monday through Thursday 11:30am to 11pm, Friday 11:30am to midnight, Saturday 11am to midnight.

Subway: 1, 2, 3, 7, 9, A, C, E, N, R (to Times Square Station). This is my all-sports-all-the-time son's favorite place to visit in Manhattan and if your son or daughter love sports, they'll love it here, too. Think: baseball, soccer, basketball, hockey, interactive games (Mad Wave Motion Theater and RPM 2 Night) and a fun restaurant, too. It's a super stimulating environment (translation: it can get nuts with lots of teens and kids), especially during the summer and school breaks. (No one under the age of 18 is allowed in the gaming room without an adult.) The restaurant doesn't take reservations and there's often a line at peak hours so think about eating when it first opens and then hitting the games (see dining section for more info). There are 200 TV's for viewing sports events but most are in the bar and lounge areas. Live radio and TV shows are often taped from here and it's not unusual to see athletes and sports celebs.

Toys 'R Us Times Square
1514 Broadway (44ᵗʰ and 45ᵗʰ), 800/869-7787, www4.toysrus.com/timessquare.
Open: Monday through Thursday 10am to 10pm, Friday and Saturday 10am to 11pm, Sunday 11am to 9pm.
Subway: 1, 2, 3, 7, 9, A, C, E, N, R (to Times Square Station).
This three-story store is big. How big? Big enough for a larger-than-life, full-size, indoor Ferris wheel. At peak times, they line up down the block for a spin on the wheel (hard to believe but true). This Toys 'R Us is atypical of the chain's other stores—if you use your imagination, think of it as a toy store/museum dedicated to Manhattan. There's a fabulous scale model of New York City landmarks in the Lego section, a life-size Barbie dollhouse and a five-ton, 20-foot-high robotic T-Rex. Tickets for the Ferris wheel are $2.50, free for kids under 2 years old. Note: Kids under 40 inches must be accompanied on the ride by an adult.

Lazer Park
163 West 46ᵗʰ Street (between Broadway and 6ᵗʰ Avenue), 212/398-3060, www.lazerpark.com.
Subway: 1,2, 3, 7, 9, A, C, E, N, R (to Times Square Station).
Open: Monday through Thursday noon to 11pm, Friday noon to 3am, Saturday 11am to 3am, Sunday 11:30am to 11pm (365 days a year).
A perfect spot for a rainy day diversion—or as a bribe to buy you time to admire the Impressionists at the Met. Young kids (seven years old and up) love to play laser tag here in the 5,000 square-foot arena, as well as the vintage arcade games, video games, pinball, BatleTech, an ultimate virtual reality game.

Madame Tussaud's New York

234 West 42nd Street, 800/246-8872, www.madame-tussauds.com.

Subway: 1,2, 3, 7, 9, A, C, E, N, R (to Times Square Station).

Open: Monday through Thursday 10am to 8pm, Friday through Sunday 10am to 10pm (open 365 days a year). Call to confirm because the museum sometimes closes early for special events.

Admission: Adults (13 to 59 years old) $25, kids (4 to 12 years old) $19, seniors (60 years and older) $22, kids under three years old are free.

Woody Allen, Joe DiMaggio, Whoopi Goldberg and Derek Jeter are all here, as well as tons of other New York-loving celebs. The first interactive wax figure was recently unveiled: a blushing Jennifer Lopez (J Lo). Whisper something to her and watch her blush (oh my God!) The "museum" features more than 200 lifesize wax figures of celebrities in theme environments, including sports, theater and entertainment. This is a great photo-op spot. Caveat: Young kids, seven and under, might be spooked by the wax effigies.

The prices are steep, but you can spend a good chunk of time here and will get your money's worth. Bonus: The film, *It Happened in NY,* a midnight ride celebrating the city's illustrious history.

MTV Studios

1550 Broadway between 44th and 45th Streets, 212/258-8000.

Subway: 1, 2, 3, 7, 9, A, C, E, N, R (to Times Square Station).

Teens gather outside this popular studio on weekdays at 3:30pm to sneak a peek of *Total Request Live* heartthrob host Carson Daly. Note: The studio is not on street level so it's hard to see much of anything. But that won't stop your teen from trying.

Parent Tip

Baseball fans, strike that, Yankees fans won't want to miss the **Yankees Clubhouse** in Times Square. Buy A-Rod and Jeter T-shirts and other cool Yankees merchandise, as well tickets to games. Let's go, Yankees!

MIDTOWN

Midtown Manhattan is a sprawling business district and home to many hotels, shops and restaurants. Midtown is all about hustle bustle. If you're out for a family stroll between noon and 2pm when the corporate world crawls out of its cubicles for air and lunch—expect impatient workers who can't believe you're actually walking *so* slowly, impeding their quick, grab-a-bite-to-eat-lunch. For seven years I worked as a travel editor at a magazine that's located at 54th Street and Fifth Avenue. My co-workers would swap horror stories about just how unbearable-and-intolerable-the-crammed-sidewalks-are-stories, especially during the holidays when tourists would clog the sidewalks to admire the stores windows dressed for the holidays and the fabulous tree at Rockefeller Center, a few blocks away. I must admit, though, I never knew what all the fuss was and actually loved the spirit of the visitors who were out and about enjoying the City that New Yorkers all too often take for granted.

Bryant Park
    40 to 42nd Street, Fifth to Sixth Avenues, 212/768-4242, www.bryantpark.org.
    Subway: F,V,B,D (to 42nd Street), 7 (to Fifth Avenue), 1,2, 3, A, C, E, N, R (to Times Square).
    Think a slice of Paris in New York. The New York Public Library's backyard, Bryant Park used to be a major drug den in the 1970's (During those years I once had to hit the pavement while walking by because of a shooting)). But, it's been cleaned up and has become one of the cities most popular parks for outdoor concerts, like the annual *Broadway Under the Stars* summer kickoff concert. The Bryant Park lawn is as big as a football field (300 feet long and 215 feet wide). Because of its midtown location, expect lots of office workers eating take-out salads and sandwiches at lunchtime on pretty spring, summer and fall days.
    The park's kinship to France is also evident in the London plane trees that are planted along the twin promenades (these are the same species of trees at the Jardin des Tuileries in Paris). Bonus: Every Monday night during the summer months, outdoor movies are shown for free. Also during the summer, *Good Morning America* hosts free Friday morning concerts in Bryant Park. And, during Fashion Week each spring you'll spy tents set up for the lineup of non-stop fashion shows.
    The real draw for young kids here is Le Carrousel, a French-inspired carousel that twirls to French cabaret music; the carousel is located mid-Park on the 40th street side. The cost: $1.75 per ride. You'll also find chess and backgammon tables, and free wireless access (if you have a laptop or handheld device). In keeping with the French theme, the game of Petangue, a French game of boules is played on a gravel path. Unique to Bryant Park is an outdoor reading room, open daily from 11am to 5pm, weather permitting.
    Combine a trip to Bryant Park with a visit to the main branch of the **New York Public Library** (there are actually 85 libraries as part of the New York Public Library system in the Bronx, Manhattan and Staten Island). This formidable building houses a dizzying collection of books, and it also is the scene for free children's workshops and storytelling hours. Before you visit Manhattan, call 212/621-0636 or visit www.nypl.org/events to request a brochure for library events that will take place during your visit.

Empire State Building

350 Fifth Avenue, 212/736-3100, www.esbnyc.com.

Open: Daily, 365 days a year, from 9:30am to midnight (last elevator leaves at 11:15pm).

Admission: $12 adults 18 years old to 61 years old, $11 seniors 62 years old and older, $11 kids 12 years old to 17 years old, $7 kids under 7 years old, free for toddlers to kids five years old. Audio tour: $5 per person.

Subway: 1, 2, 3, 9 (to Seventh Avenue), A, C, E (to 34th Street/Penn Station), B, D, F, N, Q, R (to 34th Street/Avenue of the Americas.

In a word: View. This Art Deco building on 34th Street gives visitors an eagle's eye view of Manhattan—and beyond (on a clear day, you can spy Massachusetts!). When the World Trade Center buildings stood tall, you could take in the views from the observation deck there. Now, the Empire State Building is the only gig in town. My son and I first visited the Empire State by default—kind of. One day when seven-year-old Alex was at school his beloved rabbit died suddenly. When I picked Alex up later that afternoon, I told him the sad news. I didn't have the heart—or stomach—to bring him directly home. So, I announced that we were going somewhere special—without divulging the destination, which I had no idea of as I spoke. Alex loved the anticipation and it wasn't until we were close to the Empire State building that I told him. He'd never been. We had a great time—it was a beautiful day and the views from the glass-enclosed deck with outdoor promenades on the 86th floor were stunning.

High-powered binoculars are available for a minimal cost. You'll reach the 86th floor observatory, which is 1,050 feet up by a high-speed elevator. (The 102nd floor has viewing form 1,250 feet above Manhattan, too, but recently this floor was closed to the public indefinitely.) After we soaked in the awesome view (Alex insisted he saw our house), Alex bought a King Kong key chain at the gift shop on the 86th floor and headed home. It was almost time for bed and the promise of a new day. He was still sad about his rabbit, but his first trip to the Empire State Building took the edge off. Tip: When you arrive in the city, check the local weather and plan your trip to the top of the Empire State Building accordingly—sunny, cloudless days rule.

Also make time for the Skyride attraction, a large flight stimulator that takes vistors on a sweeping aerial tour of Manhattan with James Doohan (*Star Trek's* Scotty) as the spaceship's captain.

We love the idea that you never know what colors the Empire State Building's three-tiered lighting tower will display. For instance, when the Yankees won the World Series it was lighted up in blue and white. You can even request a special color lighting for an occasion dear to your heart, keeping in mind that tons of requests are received each year. Note: Birthdays and anniversaries are not honored.

If you see the tower lights turned off during the spring or fall it could be to deter birds from flying into the building. Spring and fall are prime bird migration seasons. If a large number of birds are reported flying near the building, observatory personnel outdoor deck on the 86th floor report the sighting to the engineers who turn the lights off (birds are attracted to lights).

Bonus: The Empire State Building recently introduced an audio tour, narrated by a fictitious NYC cabbie who *tawks* about the City's landmarks, neighborhoods and attractions. The tour is available in eight languages.

Note: If you've got little ones (younger than seven or eight years old), you might want to skip New York SkyRide attraction; the lines tend to be long and the "ride" might be too frightening.

Budget Tip: You can save some bucks if you buy the ESP Observatory & New York SKYRIDE Combo Package. Purchase the package online www .esbnyc.com.

Fire Department New York Fire Zone

34 West 51st Street (between 5th and 6th avenues), 212/698-4520, www.fdnyfirezone.org www.fdnyfirezone.org (Located adjacent to Radio City Music Hall at Rockefeller Center).

Subway Stops: B, D, E, F, V.

Open: Monday through Saturday 9am to 7pm, Sundays and holidays 11am to 5pm. Note: At times the museum is taken over by school groups; call ahead to make sure it is open to the public when you'd like to visit.

Admission: $4 general, $3 kids three years old and under, free for seniors 60 years old and older.

This is an educational yet fun fire safety learning center for kids of all ages. Through a guided multi-media tour led by a firefighter, kids—and adults—learn how to crawl through a smoke-filled, dark room, feel for a hot door, identify hazards in their own home and, ultimately plan escape routes in their home.

Intrepid Sea-Air-Space Museum

Pier 86 (46th and West Side Hightway), 212/245-0072, www.intrepidmuseum.org.

Subway Stops: A, C, E. 42nd Street/Port Authority.

Open (For ships and exhibits): Fall and winter hours—Monday closed, Tuesday through Saturday 10am to 5pm, holidays 10am to 6pm. Spring and summer hours—weekdays 10am to 5pm, Saturday and Sunday 10am to 6pm, holidays 10am to 6pm.

Admission Adults $14.50; veterans/U.S. reservists/seniors/students $10.50; kids 6 to 17 years old $9.50; kids 2 to 5 years old $2.50; kids under two free.

Don't tell them it's a museum, or you're sunk. This 900-foot-long aircraft carrier is actually so *not* a museum. Tell them about the landing deck with the small planes, helicopters and jets—some of which kids can climb into. Calling all boys: below deck there's an awesome F-18 fighter jet simulator. True, there are "museumy" displays of uniforms, weapons and navy memorabilia but you can skip these and focus on the submarine *USS Growler* (guided tours only; must be at least six years old) and 25 aircraft (early wooden to supersonic jetfighters, including the *Concorde.*) Your kids will have lots of questions to ask and thankfully World War II Veterans are often on hand to oblige. Bonus: Fleet Week is held each year when more than a dozen Navy and Coast Guard ships, as well as ships from all over the globe, visit New York Harbor. There are many events, including a Parade of Ships and hours are extended.

NBC Experience Store/Studio Tours

30 Rockefeller Plaza (49th Street between 5th and 6th avenues across from Studio A, the Today Show home), 212/664-3700, www.shopNBC.com.

Subway: 47th50th streets/Rockefeller Center B, D, F, S; 49th Street N,R,W; 50th Street 1, 9.

Open Monday through Saturday: 8:30am to 5:30pm, Sunday 9:30am to 4:30pm, closed Thanksgiving and Christmas. Note: Kids under six years old not admitted.

Admission: $17.50 adults, $15 seniors and kids ages 6 to 16 years old; groups of four or more pay a $15 rate regardless of age. Note: Kids under the age of six years are not admitted.

Subway: B, D, F, Q.

Take a behind-the-scenes guided tour of the studios where *Saturday Night Live, Late Night with Conan O'Brien and Dateline NBC* are produced. Great tour for star struck visitors—you never know which anchor or celeb you'll bump into. Plus, there's neat interactive stuff: be a meteorologist and do the weather with Al Roker, test your sports trivia knowledge with sports anchor Bob Costas, or, "sit" next to Jay Leno at the *Tonight Show.* Bonus: Each interactive experience is free; you can opt to purchase a videotape.

Parent Tip

Want to wave a big hello to grandma back home in Omaha? Get up real early and head for the plaza outside of *The Today Show*'s glass enclosed studio. Katie, Matt, Ann and Al often go out to meet and greet during the live show (it starts at 7am). Bonus: Come on a Friday in the summer and catch one of the concerts. My son and I caught Ricky Martin. It's a great way to start a fabulous New York City day. (For the best view, go to the southwest corner of 49th Street and Rockefeller Center). For an up-to-date schedule of *Today* concerts, go to www.msnbc.msn.com.

෴

The NBC store on the street level floor sells NBC merchandise, including T-shirts, mugs, etc. from shows like *Friends* and *The Apprentice*. The second level houses a sweets shop—strategically situated next to where you'll line up for the tour.

SONY Wonder Technology Lab

550 Madison Avenue (56th Street), 212/833-8100, www.sonywondertechlab.com. Subway: 4, 5, 6, N, E, R.
Admission: Free (reservations recommended).
Open: Tuesday through Saturday 10am to 6pm, Thursday 10am to 8pm, Sunday noon to 6pm. Closed on Mondays and major holidays.

You'll know you've arrived by the throngs of school and camp groups. This is a popular interactive communications technology spot for kids of all ages. Bonus: The lab is located in a public atrium with a Starbucks on the street level. My office was located around the corner on 54th street and when my son would come to the office with me on school holidays we loved to come here for a hot cocoa and coffee. There's also always a hot dog/knish vendor on the corner just outside—grab a bite and take a seat at one of the many tables inside this public atrium.

The SONY attraction spans four floors of interactive experiences; there's gotta be something that'll pique your kids' interest. Even checking in is cool: a robot gives you a free, timed-entry ticket. Some of the things kids can do: jam with a musical artist at "Sony Music Video Hits," become a video editor and create a music video for Billy Joel, or visit "Medical Imaging" and become an ultrasound or endoscope specialist and explore inside the body.

Grand Central Terminal

42nd Street and Park Avenue (between Lexington and Vanderbilt Avenues), 212/532-4900, www.grandcentralterminal.com.

Built between 1903 and 1913 by a Minnesota architectural firm, this stunning train terminal is one of the City's most famous landmarks and a hotbed of activity with commuters, restaurants, shops and live entertainment. Grand Central is also tops on most tourists' must-see list.

The late Jacqueline Kennedy Onassis was Grand Central's staunchest supporter and she worked hard to save the structure from demolition that also paved the way for the legality of New York's landmark preservation law. Thanks to her help, Grand Central was restored during the 1990's. Today, it's worth a peek to see the 12-story ceiling that displays stars and the gilded constellations of the zodiac, as well as to grab a bite in the illustrious Oyster Bar where you can slurp down over 30 varieties of oysters. Steak-and-potatoes-kind-of-folks will slam-dunk at Michael Jordan's The Steakhouse; the views of the Terminal will also score points. There is a collection of stores, too. Tip: Save money by visiting the Grand Central website (listed above) and downloading discount coupons to places like Godiva chocolate that you can use when you visit. You can tour Grand Central (see tours listings), or just pop in for a stroll through. There's also a satellite branch of the New York Transit Museum (located in Brooklyn) at Grand Central. If you want to witness a quintessential New York scene, visit about 8am or 5pm on a weekday and you'll see a buzz of commuter activity.

United Nations

First Avenue to the East River, and between 42nd 48th streets (Visitor's Center located at First Avenue and 46th Street), 212/963-TOUR, www.un.org/tours.

Subway: 4, 5, 6, 7 to Grand Central Station.

Open: Tours: Monday through Friday 9:30am to 4:45pm, Saturday and Sunday 10am to 4:30pm (Closed weekends in January and February and major holidays).

Admission: $10 adults, $7.50 seniors, $6.50 students, $5.50 kids 5 years old to 14 years old, kids under 5 not admitted.

If your kids are old enough (elementary school age through teen), they'll appreciate the guided, 45-minute long tour led by young men and women representing 37 countries. The tour visits the General Assembly Hall, the chambers of the Security Council, the Social Council, and international art exhibits including tapestries and mosaics (look for the Marc Chagall stained-glass window and Norman Rockwell mosaic). You might observe a meeting in progress—an average of 5,000 meetings are held annually; of course, some are closed to the public. The U.N. actually spans 18 acres: Take a walk along the promenade, which fronts the East River; if it's late spring or summer check out the 1,400 rosebushes and sculptures donated by member nations. Which nations? Their flags fly in alphabetical order in the plaza. Your best bet for seeing delegates is to eat in the Delegates' Dining Room—if you don't see any delegates, at least you'll enjoy the view of the East River (you'll need to dress for the occasion—no shorts or sneakers and jackets are required for men.) The best time of year to experience the workings of the U.N. is when the General Assembly is in session, beginning the third Tuesday in September until late December. Another exciting time to visit the U.N. is when there are protests staged outside.

If you think your school-age child is too young to grasp the significance of a U.N. tour, think again. One guide poignantly recalls a tour she led on which there were two kids, eight and nine years old with their parents and a group of others. At one of the exhibits, she asked the group if they knew what an anti-personnel landmine was and how much did they think one would cost. None of the adults volunteered an answer and finally one of the kids said, "It costs you your life."

If you're pressed for time or have kids younger than five years old (they aren't allowed to take the tour), you can still visit the United Nations. At the Visitor's Lobby there is a free exhibit with rotating themes on display. Past exhibits have commemorated World's AIDS Day and a Children's Art Exhibit on Peace. The Visitor's Lobby is open Monday through Sunday, 9am to 5pm, March through December; during January and February it is open only Monday through Friday. To see what exhibits are being displayed while you plan to visit, go to www.un.org/events/UNART.

Parent Tip

Before you set out to visit the U.N., tell the kids you'll all be going out of the country for awhile. The United Nations is not in the United States, its is its own nation—the land belongs to all the countries that have joined the Organization. The U.N. has its own security and fire department, and even its own postage stamps. Its six official languages are: Arabic, Chinese, English, French, Russian and Spanish. Bonus: A terrific **gift shop** with items from many countries that make nice holiday gifts or souvenirs.

Rockefeller Center

47th to 52nd Streets (between Fifth and Sixth Avenues), 212/632-3975, www.rockefellercenter.com.

Subways: B, D, E, F, V.

Rockefeller Center is the core of the Big Apple. Built by the Rockefeller family in the 1930's, there are many ways to enjoy this tourist-must-see spot. Start at the Channel Gardens, which change with the seasons—during the holidays the Channel Gardens become home to a fantasy of angels. This is a perfect photo-op spot, as well as a place to sit, relax and watch the throng of tourists and office workers out for a stroll. Walk west through the gardens and you'll come to Rockefeller Plaza, anchored by the mammoth gilded statue of the Greek god Prometheus. Beneath the statue is one of the city's prettiest—and priciest—skating rinks. During Christmas the celebrated Christmas tree shadows Prometheus.

The NBC TV network is housed in the skyscraper just beyond the tree; limos pull up to drop off or pick up celeb types throughout the day. You can tour the studios; *The Today Show* tapes live at the studio to the south of the tree (see NBC Studio Tour entry). If it's a nice day, my son and I grab something delicious (soups, salads, sandwiches, pastries) to-go at Dean & DeLuca (a gourmet take-out shop) just across the street from *The Today Show* studio and eat our meal at one of the benches in Rockefeller Center. If the weather stinks, you can eat upstairs at Dean & DeLuca's—try to snag a window table that faces The Today Show studio for a celeb-spotting (of course, you may also find yourselves rubbing elbows with one at the next table). Or, opt to eat inside 30 Rockefeller Center at a handful of restaurants in the underground concourse, including such family-friendly eateries as Two Boots (Mexican). Tip: Go for it: Hit the Teuscher Chocolate shop located next to the Channel Gardens for to-die-for Swiss truffles; about $1 a pop,

Museum of Television and Radio

25 West 52nd Street (5th and 6th Avenues), 212/621-6600, www.mtr.org. Subway: E, V.

Open: Tuesday through Sunday noon to 6pm, Thursday open until 8pm. Closed Monday.

Admission: Adults $10, $8 students and seniors, $5 kids 12 years old and under. Pay-as-you-wish on Thursdays between 6pm and 8pm.

This museum is candy for couch potato kids. What kid wouldn't want to spend a couple of hours watching TV? Arrive early and reserve a tape to search and select from a huge database you'd like to view or listen to in an individual console. The Beatles on *The Ed Sullivan Show,* the last episode of *Seinfeld,* footage of man landing on the moon, it's all here—in fact, there's over 100,000 television and radio programs and advertisments that date to the 1920s. There are also ongoing workshops for kids, usually scheduled on weekends.

Museum of Modern Art

11 West 53rd Street (between 5th and 6th Avenues), 212/708-9400, www.moma.org.

Subway: E, F.

Open: call for info.

Admission: call for info.

Note: MOMA has been closed for several years to get a $650 million facelift and makeover. In the meantime, the museum was temporarily relocated to Long Island City, Queens and given the name, MOMAQNs. When this book went to press, the new MOMA in NYC was slated for a fall of 2004 opening.

Modern art lovers eagerly anticipate the grand reopening of this special museum, which will double in size. The lower level will be home to two state-of-the-art theaters. The second floor will display contemporary art exhibits, including galleries for prints and illustrated books, a media gallery and a bookstore reading room. The museum's third floor will house gallery space for architecture and design, photos, drawings and temporary exhibits. Painting and sculpture will accent the fourth and fifth floor galleries. And the sixth floor will showcase temporary exhibits in its expansive sky-lighted spaces. There will also be a fine dining restaurant and two cafes in the museum.

Parent Tips

• Got a teenage girl who balks at museums with pouty lips that have been glossed over every half-hour? Make her day with a stop at the **Sephora store** in Times Square, a giant makeup store with cosmetics from brand companies. I love browsing here. For more info, visit www.sephora.com.

• Is there an elementary age girl, six years old or older in tow? The three-story **American Girl Store** on Fifth Avenue (at 49th street, across from Rockefeller Center) is a larger-than-life dollhouse.

The New York Café here, done up in a black-and-white décor, serves meals all day for kids—and their dolls (and parents who indulge the stage their child is going through). Bonus: A treat seat for your daughter's doll. The cost for brunch is $18 per person (no, you don't have to pay for the doll) and includes cinnamon buns, French toast fruit kabobs, flower power pancakes, eggs benedict and sweet surprises (*shhh!* shortbread cookie hearts and signature chocolate mousse flowerpot). Or, opt for lunch at $20 per person which includes, a first course of fruit and cheese or vegetables with a ranch dipping sauce, a second course choice of items such as pouched salmon salad Nicoise or mini hamburger and cheeseburgers and a sweet surprises ending. Dinner at $23 per person is also offered, as is afternoon tea for $20 per person with scones and Devonshire cream, smoked salmon and cucumber sandwiches with orange fennel butter, tea sandwiches made of virginia ham and cheese, petit fours and that signature mousse flowerpot.

If your daughter is a real doll, consider taking her to theamerican Girls Revue here, a musical that brings the historical dolls to life in a 134-seat theater right in the store. The 75-minute show costs $84 a ticket (ouch!).

Get this: Visit the American Girl Store website (listed below) and plan an itinerary for your daughter and her doll. Hmm, does the doll want a new hairdo? If so, be prepared to shell out between $10 and $20.

Call 877-AG-PLACE or visit www.americangirl.com. Open: Monday through Wednesday 10am to 7pm, Thursday through Friday 10am to 9pm, Saturday 9am to 9pm and Sunday 9am to 7pm.

• Do you know who Pikachu is? If so, it's likely you've got a preschooler or elementary school age child who would love to while away some time in the **Pokemon Center** at 10 Rockefeller Plaza (at 48th Street between 5th and 6th avenues). There's a free game room on the second floor. (Can't bear the thought of it? Circumvent your way around 48th Street, the cross street where it's located.) For more information call 212/307-0900 or visit www.pokemoncenterny.com. Open: Sunday through Thursday 10am to 8pm, Friday and Saturday 9am to 9pm.

☙

FAO Schwarz
767 Fifth Avenue (at 58th Street), 212/644-9400, www.faoschwarz.com.
Subway: N, R.
Open: Monday through Saturday 10am to 7pm, Sunday 11am to 6pm.
Yes, this is a toy store, but it's one of the City's most popular tourist destinations, too. In fact, most people visit this store just to check it out, rather than buy anything—the toys are very pricey here. You'll be greeted outside by a real-life toy soldier and, if you're visiting during the holidays, expect to wait in line outside. I love the life-scale-size stuffed animals—kids love to give them a hug. Kids also love the candy department on the second floor.

Parent Tip
Steal half an hour to see the original **Winnie the Pooh animals** on display in the Central Children's room at the **New York Public Library's Donnell Branch**. This part of the library also houses tons of children's books and magazines. Located at West 53rd Street just off Fifth Avenue. Open: Monday, Wednesday, Friday noon to 6pm, Tuesday 10am to 6pm, Thursday noon to 8pm and Saturday noon to 5pm. For more information, call 212/621-0236 or visit www.nypl.org.

UPPER EAST SIDE
The City's chicest neighborhood is where you'll find pricy boutiques, restaurants and hotels, as well as a collection of fabulous museums. The real beauty of the Upper East Side is that it borders Central Park—a playground for the rich and famous who live nearby. I lived on East 83rd Street and there wasn't a day—no matter the cold temps or rainy skies—that I wouldn't run around the reservoir or walk through the park on my way to work on the West Side. Central Park is good for the soul—in a town that moves quicker than a heartbeat.
If you visit New York in early June you're in for a cultural treat. For the past 25 years, the city has celebrated a **Museum Mile Festival** held the second Tuesday in June. Nine of New York's most fabulous Fifth Avenue museums are open to visitors—free of charge. Fifth Avenue from 82nd street to 104th street is closed to traffic for a mile while live bands and street performers join in to celebrate museum day. Also during this much-anticipated event, kids can roll up their sleeves and make art. The activities vary each year but past artsy activities have included map making at the Museum of the City of New York and chalk painting in the streets.

The Metropolitan Museum of Art

Fifth Avenue (82nd Street), 212/535-7710, www.metmuseum.org. Subway: 4, 5, 6.

Open: Friday 9:30am to 9:00pm, Saturday 9:30am to 9:00pm, Sunday, Tuesday, Wednesday, Thursday 9:30am to 5:30pm, Monday closed except Columbus Day, Christmas week, Martin Luther King Jr. Day, President's Day and Memorial Day.

Admission: Suggested donation of $12 adults, $7 students and senior citizens (this includes admission to The Cloisters on the same day.) Free to children under twelve with an adult, as well as to members. Strollers are permitted during regular Museum hours, except Sundays, although many of the exhibitions can't accommodate strollers. Back carriers are available to borrow at coat check areas at the 81st and 82nd Street entrances.

Operative words for getting your kids jazzed about spending time in this art museum: mummies, tombs, The Temple of Dendur in the Egyptian wing (kids can go into parts of the Temple and throw coins into the reflecting pools that surround it), giant, colorful sculptures on the roof garden and medieval armor. If that doesn't do it, mention the Ancient Playground next door with slides, rope and tires swings, sandbox and a water sprinkler. Need more bribery, um, persuasion tips. Tell them they give you two hours at the Met and you give them a trip to the City's most outrageous candy store—Dylan's (see listing below).

You wouldn't go to Paris and skip the Louvre. Well, you shouldn't come to New York and skip The Met, simply one of the world's largest and most impressive museums with three million objects on display and incredible art exhibits. Additionally, kids ages three through seven years old (and their parents) can engage in storytelling, sketching and exploring art on many weekday afternoons and weekend mornings (call for schedule). On Friday and Saturday evenings, from 6 to 7, kids six to 12 and their parents (or grandparents) can participate in a lecture series that includes sketching. Kids can also get an activity handout at the front desk in the information lobby.

One of the coolest and most unique things about the Met is the roof sculpture garden. The views of Manhattan are super and the scene is low-key. There is a café that serves wraps and other goodies, as well as a bar. Teens will love the virgin pina coladas and strawberry dacquiris; adults will love the wine selection. The striking sculptures will wow the kids—as well as adults. Hey single parents, the Sculpture Roof Garden is apparently a good place to meet other singles.

There are several places to eat in the museum including a cafeteria-style eatery in the lower level and a more upscale restaurant on the first floor that overlooks Central Park. For coffee and dessert, the café in the American wing is a winner. However, I suggest you eat in one of the handful of good spots in the neighborhood (including The Terrace, a sidewalk café at the Stanhope

Hotel, located directly across the street). Your kids will reach a limit before they want to move on. Why not spend the time at the museum engaging in the art rather than dining?

The Solomon R. Guggenheim Museum

1071 Fifth Avenue (89th Street), 212/423-3500, www.guggenheim.org. Subway: 4, 5, 6 (86th Street).

Open: Friday through Wednesday 10am to 5:45pm, Friday open until 8pm. Closed Thursday.

Admission: $15 adults, $10 seniors and students, kids 12 years old and under are free. Friday between 6pm and 8pm is pay-what-you-wish.

Come to show the kids a beautiful Frank Lloyd Wright piece of architecture—the building itself is stunning. The collection of Picassos, Chagall, van Gogh and other important 20th century artists competes for adoration. As a kid, I loved skipping the six-story ramp that runs from the dome to the ground floor; my son loved running the same ramp (boys will be boys), so we didn't last too long here. Better suited for pre-teens, tweens and teenagers—but tell them no skateboards allowed! There's jazz in the rotunda and family flicks— check the museum's Website for current listings.

The Whitney Museum of American Art

945 Madison Avenue ((74th and 75th Streets), 800/944-8639, www.whitney.org.

Subway: 6 (77th Street).

Open: Wednesday, Thursday, Saturday and Sunday 11am to 6pm, Friday 1pm to 9pm. Closed Monday and Tuesday.

Admission: $12 adults, $9.50 seniors and students, kids 12 years old and younger are free. Pay what you wish on Friday 6pm to 9pm.

Don't let the stark institutional look intimidate you. The Whitney Museum is home to some of the best contemporary American art in the country, including a permanent collection of Edward Hopper, Jasper Johns, Georgia O'Keeffe and Roy Lichtenstein. Tweens and teenagers will appreciate this museum—and parents will enjoy sharing the experience. Be sure to pick up Family Guides in the lobby before viewing. There's also a Family Audio Guide that covers the museum's permanent collection.

Ongoing kids programs include storytelling about the art or a reading of a book by celebrated American authors—kids are encouraged to respond by drawing or sketching. Strollers are allowed in the museum, although not every exhibit. There's a wonderful and popular restaurant here, Sarabeth's, but they don't take reservations and it can get crowded.

The Frick Collection
1 East 70ᵗʰ Street (between Madison and Fifth Avenues), 212/288-0700, www.frick.org.
Subway: 6.
Open: Tuesday through Saturday 10am to 6pm, Sunday 1pm to 6pm. Friday open until 9pm. Closed Monday.
Admission: $12 adults, $8 seniors, $5 students, kids under 10 years old not admitted.

If your kids are ten years old or older, your family will enjoy stopping by this gorgeous Gilded mansion to see paintings and sculptures from the Renaissance through 19ᵗʰ century (think Rembrandt, Michelangelo and Vermeer). If your kid is an art or architecture lover, it's worth a look (although it isn't a cheap outing). Note: kids 10 and under aren't allowed.

Cooper-Hewitt National Design Museum
Smithsonian Institution, corner of Fifth Avenue and 91ˢᵗ Street, 212/849-8400, www.si.edu/ndm.
Subway: 4, 5, 6.
Open: Tuesday through Thursday 10am to 5pm, Friday 10am to 9pm, Saturday 10am to 6pm, Sunday noon to 6pm. Closed Monday, Thanksgiving, Christmas and New Years Day.
Admission: $10 adult; $7 seniors and students with ID; free for kids twelve years old and under .

The setting for this museum jewel, whose mission is to explore the impact of design in our daily lives, is the landmark Andrew Carnegie mansion. A pretty place to visit if you're in town during a spell of rainy days or frigid temps.

The Jewish Museum
1109 Fifth Avenue (92ⁿᵈ Street), 212/423-3200, www.thejewishmuseum.org.
Subway: 4, 5, 6.
Admission: $10 adults, $7.50 seniors and students. Thursday is pay-what-you-wish between 5pm and 8pm.
Open: Sunday through Thursday 11am to 5:45pm, Friday 11am to 3pm. Open Thursday until 8pm. Closed Saturdays and Jewish holidays.

"Not another museum," your kids are sure to say. Visit here on Family Fun Sundays (every Sunday, except on Jewish holidays, September through May) and they'll have faith. Dedicated to Jewish art and culture, this lovely museum features a Drop-In Arts and Crafts in the Activity Center from 1pm to 4pm for kids three and older. Ongoing arts projects that relate to the museum's permanent collection, a Jewish holiday or special exhibition engage the kids. Cost: $3 per child. There are also Family Gallery Talks on Sundays—guided tours of the galleries that are led by the museum's junior docents. Sketching in the Galleries is another exciting program for 5 to 13 year olds (free with museum admission). For really young ones (2 to 5 years old), story time is sweet (free with museum admission). The Holiday Art Cart and Archaeology Cart is a popular hands-on attraction, too.

Parent Tips

• Want to buy your little one a hip New York outfit but your kiddo doesn't have the tolerance for your shopping. Enter **DiDi's Children's Boutique**, 1196 Madison Avenue (87th Street), a toy and clothing store—with a playhouse to keep the diaper set, preschoolers and young school age kids occupied. For more information, go to www.didis.net

• Satisfy your sweet tooth at **Dylan's Candy Bar**, an outrageous—and pricey—candy store on Third Avenue at 60th Street that's owned by Ralph Lauren's daughter, Dylan. This dentist's dream is eye candy, too—towering rows of colorful candies bring a smile. The days of penny candy are history and Dylan's will cost you. Bonus: The hot fudge sundaes are made with real, oozing hot fudge. My son is a hot fudge sundae freak and he gives first prize to Dylan's. Located at 1011 Third Avenue (at 60th Street), 646/735-0078, www.dylans.com.

UPPER WEST SIDE
American Museum of Natural History

Central Park West (at 79th Street), 212/769-5100. www.amnh.org.

Open: Daily 10am to 5:45pm, The Rose Center is open late on Fridays until 8:45pm (Closed Thanksgiving and Christmas).

Admission: There are several admission policies. The museum has a suggested donation policy. However, admission to the Rose Center is $12 adults, $7 kids ages 2 to 12 years old, and $9 seniors and students. Admission to the shows at the Hayden Planetarium (and the Rose Center and the museum) are $22 adults, $13 kids (ages 2 to 12 years old), seniors/students $16.50.

Subway: 1, 9, B, C.

If your kids have patience for only one museum while visiting the City, this is the one (hopefully, though, you'll have time to take in the Metropolitan Museum of Art, as well.) The American Museum of Natural History is pleasing to kids as well as adults, with more than 45 permanent exhibition halls and special exhibitions, IMAX films, Space Shows at the Hayden Planetarium and the stunning Rose Center for Earth and Space. In the museum itself, there is a handful of exhibit halls, including the Hall of Biodiversity (rainforest diorama); Culture Hall, dedicated to anthropology; Mammals Hall (think dioramas of mammals); Hall of African Mammals; the ever-popular Fossil Halls (including two dinosaur exhibit halls that tell the story through the evolutionary process rather than chronological age); and the Milstein Hall of Ocean Life (home to the very popular 94-foot-long model of a blue whale).

Hands-down favorites of most kids, including my son: the Blue Whale and the dinosaur fossils. When Alex was in 3rd grade, his school went on a field trip to study some of the museum's dioramas and it was one of the dullest days of his life. Dioramas are cool if you look and move on, but don't expect your kids to want to linger too long at these exhibits, as his teachers expected Alex and his peers to. Kids will be happy to hang out by the dinos and whale all day, though.

You can take an hour-long tour to see five of the halls led by a museum guide (included in the price of admission). Or, spend the day exploring on your own.

The icing on the cake at the museum is the Rose Center for Earth and Space; the Space Shows take the prize. They rotate but at press time they included *Passport to the Universe,* a journey from Earth to the edge of the Universe, narrated by Tom Hanks. And *The Search for Life: Are We Alone?,* narrated by Harrison Ford.

IMAX films are another museum highlight. At press time *"Bugs! A Rainforest Adventure"* was being shown. You'll have to pay extra for IMAX movie, but your ticket will also get you into the Rose Center and the museum. IMAX ticket prices fluctuate depending on the film; check the website or call for up-to-date information.

There are also tons of family programs and workshops that take place year-round (visit the website or phone the museum for up-to-date information).

Parent Tip

If any of your children love to dance—tap, ballet, modern—*sashay* your way over to **Steps**, an incredible dance school on the Upper West Side. Take the tiny elevator to the nine studios on the upper floors (large windows allow lots of light to flood in) and watch some of New York's best dancers—as well as amateurs—plie, tap and lunge. I spent many hours here taking dance classes at Steps. Your ballerina girl or Misha-wannabe might be inspired to sign up for a class—go for it. It doesn't get any cooler than to take a dance class in a hip Manhattan dance studio. Wait 'til they tell their friends back home! Steps offers 50 open classes a day; sign up in person at the desk.

Cost: a one-hour class costs $13.50; a one-hour fitness class (Pilates, stretch and tone) costs $14.50. Located at 2121 Broadway (at 74th Street), 212/874-2410, www.stepsnyc.com.

When stomachs start rumbling, the pickings used to be slim at the Museum just several years back. That's changed. There's a food court on the lower level (sandwiches, pizza, salad bar), as well as Café Pho, which serves Vietnamese cuisine (located at the 77th Street lobby.)

Parent Tips

Here are two great food tips:

• When my son was an infant we lived directly across the street from **Café Lalo** on West 83rd Street (the Children's Museum is located a couple doors down), a sweet café with frothy cappuccinos in a setting of exposed brick walls and floor-to-ceiling windows. But the best thing about this neighborhood spot—and Hollywood set (Meg Ryan and Tom Hank's *You've Got Mail* was filmed here)—were the ceiling fans. My son was completely mesmerized by the gently whirling fans. I'd strategically sit at a table that had a primo ceiling fan view for Alex and then I'd actually *enjoy* my cup of foamy cappucino and conversation with a friend or good book.

Even if the fans aren't whirling, Café Lalo has many fans. It's a great spot for coffee and dessert (choose from more than 150 gourmet desserts). And Café Lalo also does brunch (organic cereals, steamed eggs, smoked fish, salads, Belgian waffles) from 8 am and 4 pm weekdays and between 9 am and 4 pm on weekends. Open: Monday through Thursday 8 am to 2 am, Friday 8 am to 4 am and Sunday 9 am to 2 am. Visit www.cafelalo.com.

• You haven't been to the Upper West Side if you haven't visited **Zabar's**, a sensational food store and New York landmark. Forty-thousand people a week shop here, hitting the who-knew-there-were-that-many-types-of-cheese department, the fresh fish and caviar section, and the bakery where fresh croissants march out of the ovens. Zabar's has a special place in the hearts of New Yorkers who walk, take subways and buses to shop here every week. When my son was a baby, we'd come to the store's café every morning when we lived on the Upper West Side. I'd sip my coffee and munch on one of those croissants and my infant son would win the hearts of the locals who'd stop in for a cup of java and goodie on their way to work. Bonus: Visit Zabar's and then head east a couple of blocks to Central Park to find a swath of lawn and call it a picnic! We did this often, too. Open 365 days a year, Monday through Friday 8 am to 7:30 pm; Saturday 8 am to 8 pm; Sunday 9 am to 6 pm. Located at: 2245 Broadway (at 80th Street), 212/787-2000 or visit www.zabars.com.

Children's Museum of Manhattan

212 West 83rd Street (between Broadway and Amsterdam), 212/721-1223, www.cmom.org.

Subway: 1, 9, B, C.

Open: Wednesday through Sunday 10am to 5pm. Closed Monday and Tuesday.

Admission: $6 adults, $3 seniors, kids under 1 years old free.

This five-floor museum is tucked into a neigborhood street on the Upper West Side. We lived next door to this museum and I can tell you it's a busy place with New York families on weekends, nannies with young children and school groups on weekdays and, of course, tourists. The museum can get crowded, especially on rainy days and during school holidays. Keep in mind that the museum's exhibits are skewed to younger kids, eight years old and under, with tons of interactive things for them to do, especially *really* young kids. The Word Play exhibit (for one month olds to four year olds) stimulates language development in babies and pre-schoolers, and the Early Childhood Center (for kids 18 months to 4 years old) is a safe bet for kids who love to climb, slide, paint and sing. Older kids like the interactive "TV station" and Computer Lab.

New York Historical Society

2 West 77th Street, 212/873-3400, www.nyhistory.org.

Subway: B, C.

Open: Tuesday through Sunday 10am to 6pm. Closed Monday.

Admission: $6 adults, $4 seniors and students, free for kids 12 years old and under.

The real draw for kids at this history museum is the Kid City exhibit, a re-created New York neighborhood from 100 years ago, including old-fashioned toys and household items. There are some cool things in the museum for teens, too, including George Washington's bed from Valley Forge.

The Time Warner Center Columbus Circle

Columbus Circle.

Home to one of New York's most expensive hotels (The Mandarin Oriental; see separate listing in Where to Stay section), as well as a collection of upscale restaurants and boutiques, the Time Warner Center is a welcome addition to what was once a part of town that was an eyesore.

Inside CNN

Time Warner Center Columbus Circle, 866-4CNNNYC, www.cnn.com

Subway: 1, 2, 3, A, C, B, D

Open: Monday through Saturday 1pm to 9pm, Sunday 10am to 6pm. Closed Christmas.

Admission: $15 adults, $13 seniors (65 years and older), $11 children four to 12 years old, free for children 3 years old and under.

Note: At the time this book went to press, Inside CNN was not yet open with a scheduled opening date of fall 2004.

Have a budding Barbara Walters or Tom Brokaw? A visit to this new attraction will pique his or her interest. Visitors can take 45-minute guided tours of the CNN experience. Highlighted will be the history of journalism and the CNN newsgathering process, a peek at the CNN studios and operations, a CNNfn newsroom, and a control room. Tours will depart every 10 minutes.

CENTRAL PARK

New York's jewel, Central Park is a giant playground for kids and adults, rich and poor, as well as a perennial favorite spot for tourists to visit. Of course, the warm weather months are especially great times to hang, stroll, roller blade, jog, bicycle and picnic in the Park. But most New Yorkers love to play in the Park year-round. Word to the wise: The park is not a place to hang after the sun has set, unless of course, it's summertime and you are attending one of the fabulous concerts or a Shakespeare play.

If you love to jog or run, lace up your running shoes and hit the Reservoir, a 1.58 miles dirt path that's been renamed the Jacqueline Kennedy Onassis Reservoir in recent years (it was a favorite spot of the former First Lady.) I used to run here after work every day (if the sun hadn't yet set.) Even if you aren't a runner, a stroll around the reservoir is enjoyable and the views of the Manhattan skyline are great. There are tons of kid-friendly things in the Park, including the fabulous Zoo and fun-loving Carousel.

Note: Because Central Park is so expansive, there are a number of subway lines and stations that serve it. They are:

- **West Side:**
    A, C, B, D, 1, 9 to 59th Street station
    B, C to 72nd Street station, 81st Street station and 86th Street station
- **East Side**
    N, R to 5th Avenue station
    6 to 68th Street station, 77th Street station, 86th Street station, 96th Street station, 103rd Street station and 110th Street station

Belvedere Castle/Henry Luce Observatory

Located mid-park at 79th Street, 212/772-0210, www.centralpark.org.
Open: Tuesday through Sunday 10am to 5pm.

Sitting pretty on Vista Rock, Belvedere Castle is the second highest natural elevation in the Park. In Italian, Belvedere means "panaromic viewpoint," and the views from the Castle are stunners. The Castle had suffered from years of

Parent Tip

It's a beautiful day in Central Park and your kids are happy city slickers. Then, it's time to eat but you hate to leave. What's a mom or dad to do? Do what any savvy New Yorker would do. Get out your cell phone and call **"It's a Wrap,"** a restaurant on Broadway between 68th and 69th Street that delivers bag lunches and snacks right to the playground or swath of lawn you happen to be at. Brilliant! The items on the kids menu are child-friendly and the prices are wallet friendly: Nutella De Vil, Nutella, peanut butter, granola and banana ($2.95), The Meltdown, mozzarella cheese and tomato sauce ($2.95), and Doggone It, Sabrett hot dog with or without cheese ($2.95).

For an extra $1.50, you get a 10 ounce smoothie with a kid's wrap. Gourmet wraps are available for adults. One of my favorites: the "Fuhgedaboudit," a wrap with prosciutto, salami and provolone, topped with olive relish, lettuce, tomato and lemon aioli. Call 212/362-7922 or visit www.itsawrap.com. The restaurant delivers to the following Central Park locations: 72nd and Central Park West at Strawberry Fields; Shakespeare in the Park Theater; the Bethesda Fountain (top of the steps); and Sheeps Meadow (opposite Tavern on the Green).

neglect and vandalism until 1983 when it was rescued and restored by the Central Park Conservancy. Thank you.

The Central Park Wildlife Center and Children's Zoo

839 Fifth Avenue (at 64th Street), 212/439-6500, http://wcs.org/home/zoos/centralpark.

Open: Monday through Friday 10am to 5pm, Saturday and Sunday 10am to 5:30pm and holidays 10am to 5:30pm.

Admission: Monday through Sunday $6 adults, kids 3 to 12 years old $1, seniors (65 years and older) $1.25.

The beauty of this zoo is that it's so easy to get to, thanks to its location just steps from Fifth Avenue in Central Park. The zoo is home to more than 1,400 animals of more than 130 species.

My son and my nephews' favorite parts of the zoo are watching the feeding of the seals in the sea lion pool. Feeding time is 11:30am, 2pm and 4pm. Also a kick is the penguin feeding at 10:30am and 2:30pm. The polar bear exhibit is also really cool.

The Tisch Children's Zoo here is especially popular with the diaper crowd. Goats, sheep, a cow and a Vietnamese potbellied pig will tug at the littlest ones hearts. Kids can feed these animals (you can buy a handful of food for 25 cents from a dispenser). Kids also giggle when they "pet" the bronze animal sculptures that are located next to each pen and a squeak or squawk is emitted. The Enchanted Forest is centrally located in the Zoo. There is an aviary with live turtles, frogs and birds and a children's theater (there are two theaters in the Zoo, the other is located in the central courtyard.) Daily shows about animals are performed daily for kids.

And don't miss the George Delacorte Musical Clock, located between the Wildlife Center and the Children's Zoo. Every hour on the hour one of 32 nursery rhyme tunes plays while a bear with tambourine, a hippopotamus with violin, a goat with pan pipes, a kangaroo and offspring with horns, and a penguin with drum parade around the base of the clock. The animals give a shorter performance on the half-hour. When my son was little he adored this.

Bonus: Take a free tour led by wildlife guides, every Tuesday at 2:30pm. The tour meets at the penguin exhibit. Note: Advance reservations are required; call the number above.

And here's another bonus: If your kids are nocturnal like mine (my son thinks sleep is a complete waste of time), why not join the other nocturnal creatures at the Central Park Zoo on an overnight sleepover. Yep, you sleep inside the zoo! Snooze at the Zoo is offered three times a year between October and February. The program is educationally skewed: kids make crafts, learn about some of the animal habitats and watch the zookeepers at work preparing the animal's breakfast. Cost: $160 each adult/child pairing. For more information or to make reservations, call 212/459-6583.

The Harlem Meer

106th to 110th eastside, 212/860-1370, www.centralparknyc.org.

This lovely body of water (*meer* is Dutch for "lake") in the upper northern reaches of the Park has been restored to become a spectacular, rugged setting. The 11-acre meer is stocked with bass, catfish, shiners and bluegills. One of the most popular things for families (kids and adults) here is the catch-and-release fishing program. The Dana Discovery Center (see next entry)

Parent Tip

You don't necessarily have to travel to Yankee or Shea Stadiums to take in a ball game and hot dogs. The **New York Gotham Baseball Club** reenacts games played the way they were in 1864 on the **Great Lawn** in Central Park throughout the summer. Remember, New York City is where the game was invented (well, that's one theory anyway). For a game schedule and more info go to www.zyworld.com/gothambaseball. Tip: There are dozens of hot dog vendors throughout the park.

☙

supplies the poles, unbarbed hooks (remember, this is a catch-and-release program) and instruction booklets. The catch-and-release program takes place Tuesdays through Saturdays, mid-April to mid-October, 10am to 4pm. (the last pole is handed out at 3pm). Note: Children under 14 years old must be accompanied by an adult. Cost: Free with a current photo ID.

Bonus: Visit at Halloween for the pumpkin sail of candlelit Jack o' Lanterns across the meer.

The Charles A. Dana Discovery Center

Located at 110th Street and Lenox Avenue inside the Park, on the northern shore of the Harlem Meer, 212/860-1370, www.centralparknyc.org.

Open: Tuesday through Sunday 10am to 5pm.

Central Park's newest building, which opened in 1993, is one of four visitor centers in the Park; this one serves Upper Park visitors. It's also the place for the Central Park Conservancy's free family and community events. The Great Hall here, host to collaborative exhibits with City museums and other institutions, has a small deck that overlooks the Meer and views of the Park's southern environs. Bonus: Jazz concerts and other performance festivals and fun events are also staged here.

The Loeb Boathouse

Located on the East Side between 74th and 75th Streets, www.centralparknyc.org.

Rowboat rentals: March through October, daily 10am to 5pm (weather permitting). Cost: $10 first hour and $2.50 each additional 15 minutes (a $30 cash deposit is required).

Bicycle Rentals: Cost: $9 to $15 per hour (credit card, driver's license or passport required).

A favorite spot of adults and children, this is the unspoken central headquarters of the park. There are many things you can do here: Rent rowboats (up to five people per boat) or take a Venetian gondola ride on the lake. Rent bicycles at the bicycle rental concession for a spin in the park. Enjoy some snacks on the outside terrace or dine at the restaurant, which overlooks the lake and has a deck with overhead heating so you can sit outside. We have spent many long afternoons enjoying the New York scene here.

The Ramble

Located mid-park from 73rd to79th streets, to the west of the entrance of the Boathouse, www.centralparknyc.org.

New Yorkers love this 3.8 acre "wild garden" that was created (only the bedrock existed, everything else was made). Twenty-six species of butterflies make their home here, as well as 320 bird species. There's a tumbling stream called "The Gill." Note: There are sections that are fenced off as part of efforts to preserve the land.

Conservatory Garden

Located mid-park from 104th to 106th streets on the east side (enter at Fifth Avenue and 105th street or at the 106th street gate inside the Park.

A lovely, six-acre formal garden that takes its name from the glass conservatory that once stood here. There are actually three separate gardens, each representing different styles: Italian, French and English. The gardens features bronze sculptures, fountains and, of course, shrubs and flowers.

Sheep Meadow

Located on the west side, mid-park between 66th and 69th streets.

Open: May to mid-October, dawn to dusk (weather permitting).

New Yorkers love this giant—15 acres—grassy space. If the sun is shining and the temps are warm, this expanse of velvet green is spot on for sunbathing and picnics. We used to see John F. Kennedy Jr. here throwing his Frisbee. Bonus: Lilac Walk, on the northern edge of Sheep Meadow, features 23 different varieties of lilacs from around the globe. A much-revered slice of paradise in a concrete jungle of a city.

Strawberry Fields

Located on the west side between 71st and 74th streets.

This teardrop shaped piece of land honors John Lennon of the Beatles, who was killed across the street in front of his apartment building, the Dakota (72nd street and Central Park West). Strawberry Fields is named after the Beatles song *Strawberry Fields Forever.* Lennon's wife, Yoko Ono, donated $1 million to the Central Park Conservancy to landscape and maintain the park and countries from all over the globe donated trees.

Whenever we come here there is always at least one person playing guitar while sitting near the black-and-white mosaic design which reads IMAGINE, the title of one of Lennon's songs. Often, there is impromptu singing of Beatles

Parent Tip

A popular way to see Central Park year-round is by **horse-drawn carriage**. These rides have been around forever; I took a horse-drawn carriage ride on my prom night (smooch.) That was the last time, as I feel sorry for the horses who jockey for space with cabs and other traffic. But these rides are enormously popular with romantics and families alike. You'll see the carriages lined up at the southern end of the Park along Central Park South (beginning at 59th Street, across from FAO Schwarz and the Plaza Hotel) between Fifth and Sixth avenues. Cost: $34 for the first 20 minutes and $54 for a 45 to 50 minute tour. Call 212/736-0680 for more information.

☙

songs by visitors who also light candles and place flowers on the mosaic as a tribute to Lennon. It's a quiet, reflective and humbling spot in the middle of a bustling city that Lennon adored. When George Harrison died, Strawberry Fields was packed with Beatles' fans who gathered to sing and reflect.

As you stroll this peaceful part of the park, you'll come across a bronze plaque that lists the 121 countries that endorse Strawberry Fields as a Garden of Peace.

The Dairy

Located mid-park at 65th Street, 212/794-6564.

Open: Tuesday through Sunday 10am to 5pm.

Once upon a time, in the 19th century, children would be rewarded in the Park with a glass of fresh milk from this quirky Victorian building. One side of the building is an open loggia, made of wood with geometric gingerbread trim. The other side is made of granite with spires that are reminiscent of a country church. The view from the Dairy is quintessential New York: Wollman Rink with the skyline as a backdrop.

You can't get a glass of milk here any longer though. Today, the building houses a Visitor Center where you can pick up brochures and maps and gather information about the history of Central Park, as well as events that are taking place in the Park. The Dairy is also the Park's official gift shop.

Look west of the Dairy and you'll spy what is called "children's mountain," a large bedrock outcrop on which the brick Chess and Checkers House stands. There are 24 shaded chess tables and players come from all over to play here.

Carousel

Located mid-park at 64th Street, 212/879-0244.

Open: Daily April through November 10am to 6pm (weather permitting), Weekends November through April 10am to 4:30pm (weather permitting). Cost: $1 per ride.

No trip to Manhattan is complete without a spin on this vintage carousel, one of the largest carousels in the country with 58 hand-carved painted horses. Makes for sweet memories.

The Great Lawn

Located mid-park from 79th to 85th streets.

Eureka! If you are visiting the City in the summer, you must take in one of the City's most treasured pleasures: an evening concert by the New York Philharmonic or the Metropolitan Opera, each of which performs twice. The performances complement the Manhattan skyline views for an evening of New York magic. You'll share this 55-acre Crayola green swath of lawn with about a million New Yorkers, so it's best to stake out your blanket territory early in the day. You won't be alone. New Yorkers are very territorial and many arrive at dawn to stake their claim. New Yorkers also know how to plan a gourmet picnic—you won't believe some of the elaborate spreads: champagne, pates, lobster, candelabras.... You certainly won't want to look like a tourist so plan to bring a picnic yourselves.

Your best bets for picnic fare are: Visit Zabar's on the Upper West Side to create your own picnic (see sidebar).

Alice in Wonderland Statue

Located East 74th Street, north of the Conservatory Water.

Little girls especially love to pay a visit to Alice and her entourage from the Lewis Carroll classic Alice's Adventures in Wonderland. There's the Mad Hatter, the March Hare, and the Cheshire Cat. The sculpture by Jose de Creeft was commissioned by philanthropist George Delacorte to honor his wife, Margarita. Kids aren't drawn to the sculpture as much to admire it as to climb and explore its many surfaces and textures.

Bethesda Fountain

Located mid-park at 72nd Street.

This fountain is a great meeting spot, as well as a perfect spot to wile away some down time. An angel adorns the fountain's center. And there's usually always someone strumming a guitar or humming a harmonica.

Swedish Cottage Marionette Theatre

Located on the west side at 79th Street, you must make reservations, 212/988-9093.

Show times: Tuesday through Friday 10:30am and noon, Saturdays 1pm. Closed Sundays, Mondays and school and national holidays.

Admission: $6 adults, $5 children (suggested).

Jack in the Beanstalk, Cinderella and Hansel and Gretel are part of the repertoire of the marionette theater company that performs here. They write or adapt their own scripts, as well as construct and costume the puppets. They recently performed a new production called The Princess, the Emperor and the Duck, based on The Princess and the Pea, The Emperor's New Clothes and The Ugly Duckling. Productions rotate so call to see what will be playing when you are visiting.

Parent Tip

The **Central Park Conservancy** offers many free programs throughout the year for kids of all ages. For an up-to-date listing go to the Central Park Conservancy's website at www.centralparknyc.org. Note: You must register for these events.

☙

ELLIS ISLAND
The Statue of Liberty

Liberty Island, 212/363-3200, www.nps.gov/stli.

Ferry: Circle Line ferry leaves Battery Park every hour on the hour daily. Round trip ferry cost: $10 kids and adults 13 years old and older, $8 seniors, $4 kids ages 3 to 12 years old, free kids 2 and under. You can purchase advance tickets by phone: 866/STATUE or 212/269-5755 outside the U.S. and Canada. You can also purchase advance tickets online. Ferries depart from New York City's Battery Park (212/269-5755) and Jersey City's Liberty State Park (201/435-9499).

Subway to the ferry: 1, 9.

Open: 9:30am to 5pm, although the hours are adjusted seasonally. Closed on Christmas.

Note: If you're short for time, the ferry from Manhattan stops first at the Statue of Liberty on its way to Ellis Island. You can disembark and catch a later ferry to Ellis Island. Or, you can take your photos from the boat and just continue onto Ellis Island.

The Statue of Liberty interior and museum has been closed to visitors since September 11, 2001, although the grounds were open for strolling and viewing the statue. However, at press time, news came that the Statue would reopen to visitors in the summer of 2004 following a multi-million dollar renovation, primarily for security upgrades. According to the NYC & Company Convention & Visitors Bureau, the museum will reopen and, while visitors will still not be able to enter the interior of the Statue, including the crown, they will be able to view the Statue's interior through a glass ceiling near the statue's base. Visitors will also be able to go to the observation deck on top of the 16-foot pedestal to see the 360-*degree view.* (Prior to 9/11, visitors were able to climb the 354 steps to the Statue's crown or 192 steps to the top of the pedestal.)

It goes without saying that security will be extremely tight and you should anticipate a wait, even though there are plans to launch a new reservations ticketing system to reduce the wait time. For current information, go to www.nps.gov/stli.

The Statue of Liberty National Monument was a gift from the people of France to the people of the United States more than 100 years ago (she celebrated her 100th birthday in 1986) as a gesture of friendship between the two nations during the American Revolution. Through the years, the Statue has become a symbol of freedom and democracy and has welcomed many immigrants to this country.

A visit to the Statue of Liberty is an enriching and educational experience for kids. To enhance the visit, sign up for the Junior Ranger Program, a self-guided program for kids ages 7 to 12 (this is a recommended age range, but younger and older kids can also participate). Keep in mind for really young kids, getting to Lady Liberty really is half the fun—or the whole fun in the case of the salty, windy, sunny ferry ride over. The kids get a Junior Park Ranger Booklet that teaches them about the importance of the National Park Service and the Statue of Liberty through kid-friendly activities. The booklet takes about one hour to complete. They can download the booklet at www.nps.gov/ stli or pick one up at the Information Center on Liberty Island. Activity sheets are also available for kids free or charge; you can pick them up from park rangers at the information center.

There is more to the Statue of Liberty than the monument. There are also several museums on site. Located on the second floor of the pedestal is the Statue of Liberty Exhibit, which traces the history of the Statue through photos, videos and oral presentations. Kids will love the full-scale replicas of the Statue's foot and face that are on display here. There are also exhibits that explore the symbolism of the Statue. And a bronze plaque with the "New Colossus," a famous sonnet written by Emma Lazarus in 1883, is also housed here; Lazarus contributed to the completion of the Statue's pedestal.

The Torch Exhibit features the original 1886 torch and flame in the lobby, and a complementary exhibit on the balcony's second floor that details the history of the torch.

A visit to Ellis Island is interesting for school age kids and older. Twelve million immigrants passed through here between 1892 and 1954. In 1990, Ellis Island opened as a museum there.

A really cool, worthwhile thing to do: have your ancestors names inscribed on the American Immigration Wall of Honor at Ellis Island. Note: Your relatives did not have to come through Ellis Island to this country; as long as they immigrated to the U.S. their names can be inscribed on the wall. You can do this either online (go to www.wallofhonor.com) or when you arrive. My mother had my grandparents names (John and Christina Mackinnon MacDougall, Scotland) and (Santa and Anna Freni, Italy) inscribed on the Wall. Cost: $100 each name. For more information call Donor Service at 212/561-4500.

There is a cafeteria that sells sandwiches and snacks. But, if you plan ahead, you'll grab a couple of pastrami or corned beef deli sandwiches in Manhattan before jumping on the ferry; there are plenty of perfect-picnic-perches on Liberty Island and Ellis Island.

Fun Facts:
• The length of Lady Liberty's index finger is 8 feet.
• The length of her hand is 16 feet and 5 inches.
• The length of her nose is 4 feet and 6 inches.
• The length from the ground to the tip of her torch is 305 feet and one inch.
• The thickness of her waist is 35 feet.

- There are 25 windows in her crown to symbolize gemstones found on the earth and the heaven's rays. The seven rays in the crown are representative of the seven seas and continents of the world.
- The Statue of Liberty is a Leo (kidding.)

Chapter 7

THE OUTER BOROUGHS

QUEENS
Flushing Meadows Corona Park
Long Island Expressway (Roosevelt Avenue Van Wyck Expressway—111th Street, 718/271-1500 www.flushingmeadowscoronapark.org.
Subway: No. 7 to 111th Street or Willets Point/Shea Stadium.
Train: Long Island Rail Road (LIRR).
Open: Seven days 10am to 5pm, all year round.
Admission: $5 adults, $1 kids, $1.25 seniors.
This enormous 1,255-acre park, which once hosted the 1939 and 1964 World's Fair is home to many attractions, including an art museum, a science museum, a botanical garden, a baseball stadium, two lakes (one accessible), a miniature golf course and a pitch-and-putt golf course (see golf listings). The park's centerpiece is the Unisphere, a 140-foot-tall, stainless steel ball that was presented to the 1964 World's Fair by U.S. Steel. You can picnic and play in the park (see parks listings) or, visit the following attractions.

Queens Museum of Art
Flushing Meadows Corona Park, 718/592-5555, www.queensmuseum.org.
Subway: 7 to Willets Point/Shea Stadium.
Train: LIRR.
Open: September to June, Wednesday through Friday 10am to 5pm, Saturday and Sunday noon to 5pm; during July and August the museum is open Wednesday through Sunday from 1pm to 8pm. Closed major holidays.
Admission: (suggested donation) $5 adults, $2.50 seniors and kids.

The main reason you'll want to visit this museum: The Panorama of the City of New York, the world's largest architectural scale model, is really cool for kids (and our friend Larry Martone who absolutely loves this exhibit). Originally constructed for the 1964 World's Fair, this 9,335-square-foot replica of New York City includes more than 900,000 buildings. This is a mind-boggling exhibit for kids.

The Queens Botanical Garden

43-50 Main Street, Flushing, 718/886-3800, www.queensbotanical.org.

Subway/Train: 7 subway or Long Island Rail Road/ Port Washington line to Main Street-Flushing. Take the Q44 bus or walk south 8 blocks.

Open: Spring/summer hours—the month of March open Tuesday through Sunday 8am to 4:30pm; April through September, open Tuesday through Friday 8am to 7pm. Closed Mondays.

Admission: Free (donations are welcome).

A pretty Japanese Garden is one reason to visit the 39-acre garden. The other reason: the price is right.

New York Hall of Science

47-01 111th Street (at 48th Avenue), Flushing Meadows-Corona Park, 718/ 699-0005, www.nyscience.org.

Subway: 7 to 111th Street, then walk three blocks south.

Open: Summer hours—Monday 9:30am to 2pm, Tuesday through Friday 9:30am to 5pm, Saturday and Sunday 10:30am to 6pm. Fall/Winter/Spring hours—Tuesday through Thursday 9:30am to 2pm, Friday 9:30am to 5pm, Saturday and Sunday noon to 5pm Closed Mondays except holidays.

Admission: Adults (ages 18 years old and older) $9, children (5 to 17 years old, college with ID) $6, Preschoolers (2 to 4 years old) $2.50, Senior citizens (ages 62 and older) $6. Note: Free admission is offered Fridays between 2 and 5pm (September 1 through June 30). Science playground fees: $3 per person, $2 for group (the playground is open March through December, weather permitting, to children of all ages with adult supervision). Strollers are permitted.

Slides, seesaws, more than two-dozen playground elements—with an educational bent (gravity, motion, etc.)—attract kids to the indoor-outdoor Science Playground here. There are also 225 hands-on exhibits, as well as deftly-performed cool science demonstrations throughout this Queens museum. Exhibits include teen-friendly stuff like the recent Sports Science Summer; kids test their skills at interactive sports like basketball, tennis, and surfing and then see how they can improve by applying the laws of science.

The Queens Zoo

53-51 111th Street at 53rd Avenue, Flushing Meadows Corona Park. 718/271-1500, www.wcs.org.

Open: Monday through Friday 10am to 5pm, Saturday and Sunday 10am to 5:30pm, holidays 10am to 5:30pm (open 365 days a year).

Admission: Adults $5, kids (3 to 12) $1, seniors (65 years and older) $1.25.

Subway: 7 to 111th Street, then walk a couple of blocks south to 46th Avenue.

More than 400 animals call this 11-acre zoo home sweet home. If you're really into zoos and have time to check out all of the zoos in the area, pay a visit. Otherwise stick with the Central Park Zoo or Bronx Zoo.

The American Museum of the Moving Image

35th Avenue at 36th Street, Astoria, 718/784-4520, www.ammi.org. Subway: N, W,.R, G.

Open: Wednesday, Thursday 11am to 5pm, Friday 11am to 7:30pm, Saturday and Sunday 11am to 6:30pm. Friday through Sunday there are extended hours for screenings. Closed Mondays (except holidays) and Tuesday.

Admission: $10 adults, $7.50 seniors and students, $5 kids between five years old and 18 years old

Kids who love television and the movies will enjoy this museum that houses a collection of costumes, cameras and props. The museum is also hands-on for kids interested in the movie making process. It also screens movies and is the site for celebrity-studded events. Bonus: Vintage video arcade games like PacMan that visitors can play.

Queens County Farm Museum

73-50 Little Neck Pkwy (Union Turnpike and Grand Central Parkway), Floral Park, Queens, 718/347-FARM, www.queensfarm.org.

Subway: E or F train to Kew Gardens/Union Tpke Station or take the Port Washington branch on the Long Island Rail Road (LIRR) to Little Neck Station.

Open: Monday through Friday 9am to 5pm, year-round (outdoor visiting only); and Saturday and Sunday 10am to 5pm tours of the historic farmhouse are given.

Admission: Free.

A working historical farm that's a short-term diversion for kids—if you're in the neighborhood. Otherwise, opt for Manhattan's Central Park or Bronx zoos if it's animals you want to see in an enriching setting. Caveat: You need a car to reach here. Bonus: It's a free attraction.

Shea Stadium

126th Street & Roosevelt Avenue, Flushing, Queens, 718/507-8499, www.mets.com.

It's easy to get to the Stadium from Manhattan. By subway, take the #7 train to Willets Point/Shea Stadium. It's a quick five minute walk from the station to the stadium. You can also take the Long Island Rail Road from Penn Station; take the Port Washington line (this line makes stops at Shea on game days only.) Or, take the NY Waterway Shea Express; roundtrip tickets cost $17 adults, $13 children 12 years old and under. The boats depart from Pier 11 (Wall Street), East 34th Street and East 90th Street; call 800/53-FERRY or visit www.nywaterway.com.

This ballpark that's home to the Mets doesn't have the same allure as its rival stadium in the Bronx (Met fans may take exception to my saying so). Still, the ball club is beloved by millions of New Yorkers and Long Islanders and packs 'em in for games. If you're in town for one of the "subway series" games between the Yankees and Mets, you'll see Shea Stadium filled to the rafters. Originally, the stadium was to be called Flushing Meadow Park, thanks to its location in Flushing Meadows-Corona Park. But the stadium was renamed as a tribute to William Shea, the gentleman who was responsible for bringing the National League back to the City. A fun-loving, New York baseball stadium.

Parent Tip

If the Mets are in town and you want to see a day game, combine a visit to Shea Stadium with a visit to one of the **Flushing Meadows-Corona Park** attractions listed above. It's easy to do. You'll take the Number 7 train to the Shea Stadium stop—the subway stop for both Shea and Flushing Meadows. Note: The same tip applies if you are visiting around Labor Day when the U.S. Open is at the **USTA National Center**, a baseball throw away from Shea Stadium and the Park's exhibits.

‏‏‎ ‎⁓

Socrates Sculpture Park

Broadway at Vernon Blvd., Long Island City, 718/956-1819, www.socratessculpturepark.org.

Open: 10am to sunset year-round.

Admission: Free.

Subway: N or W Train to Broadway stop in Queens, then walk eight blocks toward the East River.

Queens' residents are very proud of this park and outdoor museum, which they adore for its contemporary sculpture and East River views. Bonus: Kids can climb the structures. If you are visiting in June, the Summer Solstice Festival is special, with storytelling and face painting for children.

STATEN ISLAND
Staten Island Children's Museum
1000 Richmond Terrace, Snug Harbor Cultural Center, 718/273-2060.
Open: Tuesday through Sunday noon to 5pm.
Admission: $5 adults and kids, free for kids two years old and under.
Getting There: Take the Staten Island ferry and then board the S40 bus to Richmond Terrace.

There are eight exhibits at this small museum with some cool stuff for little tykes like water play and bugs (feeding time for the little critters is at 3pm). Kids can also play dress-up in Portia's Playhouse and be a good neighbor in Mister Roger's Neighborhood. You'll especially appreciate the lovely setting at the Snug Harbor Cultural Center with picnic tables that beckon picnickers.

Staten Island Zoo
614 Broadway, Staten Island, 718/442-3100, www.statenislandzoo.org.
Open: Daily 10am to 4:45pm.
Admission: $5 adults, $4 seniors, $3 children, free kids four-years-old and under.

Teeny compared to the rambling Bronx Zoo (and less crowded than the Central Park Zoo), this eight-acre zoo isn't about elephants and rhinos. Instead, it home to huge monkeys, snakes, lizards, leopards and antelope and other similarly-placed animals on the survival-of-the-fittest spectrum. Bonus: A small-scale aquarium and kids weekend workshops. Still, if you want to see just one zoo while in the City, opt for the Central Park Zoo or Bronx Zoo.

Getting there: Take the Staten Island Ferry (free) to the St. George ferry Terminal where you'll board the S48 bus to Forest Avenue and Broadway. Make a left on Broadway and continue walking a few blocks until you spy the zoo's entrance.

BROOKLYN
Brooklyn Botanic Garden
900 Washington Avenue (across from Prospect Park), 718/623-7200, www.bbg.org.
Subway: Q train to Prospect Park Station (note: the B train doesn't run on weekends) or the 2 or 3 train to Eastern Parkway.
Open: April through September Tuesday through Friday 8am to 6pm; weekends and holidays 10am to 6pm; closed Mondays (except holidays that fall on Mondays, but not Labor Day). October through March Tuesday through Friday 8am to 4:30pm; weekends and holidays 10am to 4:30pm. Closed

Monday, Thanksgiving, Christmas and New Year's Day (open Mondays that fall on a holiday).

Admission: $5 seniors, $3 students, kids under 16 years old are free. Note: Admission is free Saturday 10am to noon and all day Tuesday; seniors are free Fridays, too.

A 52-acre jewel in Brooklyn—with a twist. There's the sweet fragrance garden for the blind. And a celebrity path with the names of famous Brooklynites: think Woody Allen and Mae West. Daffodil Hill is awash in yellow each spring followed closely by a brushstroke of pink when the cherry blossoms that ring the Japanese Pond explode with color. The Cranford Rose Garden bursts into bloom early each summer, and when the gardens are frosted in white come winter, you can visit the indoor Steinhardt Conservatory, a showplace for orchids. Kids can see how green their thumbs are at the Discovery Garden, a 13,000-square-foot center designed for budding botanists with hands-on activities. Kid's workshops are also offered on weekends.

Parent Tip

The **Heart of Brooklyn Trolley** stops at many Brooklyn attractions, including the Brooklyn Children's Museum. The trolley operates on Saturday, Sunday and holidays from noon to 6pm. Also, the BCM (Brooklyn Children's Museum) Trolley Express runs every hour (between 10:15am and 4:15pm) on weekends from the Grand Army Plaza.

New York Aquarium at Coney Island

Surf Avenue (and West 8th Street), Brooklyn, 718/265-FISH, www.nyaquarium.com.
Subway: D train to Stillwell Avenue Station in Coney Island.
Open: Daily 10am to 5pm.
Admission: $11 adults, $7 seniors and kids.

The daily sea lion shows are worth the price of admission alone. You'll also fall in love with the walruses. All told, there are 300 species of sea life in this 14-acre aquarium. My son's Greenwich Village camp took a field trip here and it was one of the highlights of his summer. Translation: Expect lots of summer camp groups to share the space in the summer during your visit.

Brooklyn Children's Museum

145 Brooklyn Avenue (at St. Marks Avenue), www.bchildmus.org.
Subway: A or C train to High Street (first stop in Brooklyn).
Open: Wednesday through Friday 1pm to 6pm, Saturday and Sundays 11am to 6pm. Closed Monday and Tuesday and Thanksgiving, Christmas and New Year's Day. Note: Admission is free the first Thursday of each month and Saturdays/Sundays before noon—otherwise admission is $4.

The first and oldest children's museum in the country (founded in 1899), the Brooklyn Children's Museum has also made its mark as one of the best kid's museums around. Kids love to enter the museum through the neon-lighted tunnel. A Totally Tots area is dedicated just to the preschool set. Older kids dig the TV and video stuff. And animals and plants get a lot of attention at this museum with special programs and activities. Bonus: There's an outdoor area for kids to run around—weather permitting.

New York Transit Museum

Corner of Boerum place and Schermerhorn Street in Brooklyn Heights, www.mt.nyc.ny.us/mta/museum.

Admission: $5 adults, $3 seniors and kids three years to 17 years old.

Open: Tuesday through Friday 10am to 4pm, Saturday through Sunday noon to 5pm, closed Monday and holidays.

Many kids love trains—my son was obsessed with them when he was real young. This museum, the largest in the country devoted to urban public transportation history, has been renovated in recent years and makes its home in a decommissioned 1936 Brooklyn. subway station. You'll learn the history behind the City's subway system (yawn), board vintage subway and elevated trains and visit a working signal tower. The newer additions especially jazz kids—buses they can board and a simulated traffic intersection with traffic lights and coordinated walk/don't walk signs, parking meters and fire hydrants. The museum has created a Website that invites visitors to share transit stories (the LIRR should only be so obliging) and photographs and even view some exhibits. Again, this is a fun museum—if you dig trains and buses.

DUMBO

DUMBO is not a flying elephant (although really young children will prefer it were). DUMBO is the acronym for Down Under the Manhattan Bridge Overpass, located at the heel of the Brooklyn Bridge, just five minutes from lower Manhattan. DUMBO is home to a very cool, progressive arts community, as well as a selective collection of eateries, shops and pricey residences.

The views of Manhattan from DUMBO are works of art in of themselves: the Statue of Liberty, the Brooklyn and Manhattan bridges and the Manhattan skyline. There's a park that sits pretty along the river—grab a hot cocoa from Jacque Torres Chocolate shop and sit at this riverfront perch to soak in the intoxicating views (see listing below). Retailers include ABC Home and West Elm and new ones pop up practically overnight.

A heads-up for ice cream lovers: One of my closest friends, who has lived in nearby Brooklyn Heights for about ten years, insists that the best ice cream is at the Brooklyn Ice Cream Factory at Fulton Ferry Landing (between Old Fulton and Water streets; 718/246-3963.) There are only eight flavors to choose from, (refreshing in itself), especially for kids who are prone to meltdowns when bombarded with too many choices.

Parent Tip

Jacques Torre Chocolate:
66 Water Street, between the Brooklyn and Manhattan bridges, 718/875-9772, www.mrchocolate.com.
Open: Monday through Saturday 9am to 7pm.
Chocolate lovers die and go to heaven every day here. You can buy chocolates to go or have a seat at one of the café tables and sip hot cocoa and munch on pain au chocolats. Bonus: Torre uses no preservatives and only natural ingredients.

Grimaldi's Pizzeria:
19 Old Fulton Street (under the Brooklyn Bridge), 718/858-4300.
Open: Sunday through Thursday 11:30am to 10:45pm, Friday 11:30am to 11:45pm and Saturday noon to 11:45pm.
Think red-checkered tablecloths and out-of-this-world pizza thin crust pizza that's made in coal brick ovens.

BRONX

Yes, the Bronx is up—uptown that is. And it's home to one of the city's most celebrated landmarks, Yankee Stadium, as well as the world-famous Bronx Zoo.

We're frequent visitors to the Bronx to see the Yankees play. And there's no better place in October than in the Bronx. Forget leaf peeping in New England, if the Yankees are in the World Series, this is the best spot to appreciate the crisp autumn air.

The Bronx gets a bad rap (no pun intended as this is also where rap music is enjoyed on the streets and in clubs) as being a place where you shouldn't go. But if you know where to go in the Bronx, you'll discover it to be a vibrant part of the fabric of the City.

In fact, while most people envision the Bronx to be a giant maze of concrete, the Bronx actually has more parkland than in any of the other boroughs, including the incredible New York Botanical Garden—250 acres that include 27 specialty gardens and a stunning 50-acre forest. Wave Hill, a pretty public garden and cultural institution is also in the Bronx.

Of course, the Bronx Bombers who play at Yankee Stadium call this borough home. As do the 4,000 animals that live at The Bronx Zoo, the largest urban zoo in the country dating back to 1899. And many celebs have lived here including Tony Curtis, Ann Bancroft, Regis Philbin, Lou Gehrig, Edgar Allan Poe (you can visit his house), Mark Twain, John F. Kennedy and Ralph Lauren. Settled in 1639 and named for Swedish settler, Jonas Bronck, the Bronx has about 60 historic sites and landmarks (several are listed below).

Yankee Stadium
161st Street and River Avenue, 718/293-6000, www.yankees.com.
Subway: 4, B, D to 161st street which is directly at Yankee Stadium.
Ferry: New York Waterway, 800/53-FERRY, www.nywaterway.com.
The House that Ruth Built is one of the city's most famous landmarks. It is also, in some ways, a shrine to the legacy of the Yanks—and the history of baseball—even for those of you who aren't Yankee fans (you know who you are) but love the game.

The Stadium opened on April 18, 1923 when the Yankees played against, who else, the Red Sox. The rest, as they say, is history. The Yankees have gone on to win 26 championships (at press time; hopefully 27 by the time this book comes out).

Most Major League Baseball players—and fans—agree that there is an unexplained mystique when playing at this ballpark. Baseball fans, too, appreciate a game played here. We've been to many ballparks, but there's something magical about watching a game at Yankee Stadium. Lots of families even plan their vacation to the City when the Yankees will be in town; check the Yankee's home game-schedule at www.yankees.com.

We're big baseball fans and especially love the Yankees. My son's father was drafted by the Yankees when he was in college. (My great-grandfather and great-uncle both played in the Major Leagues for 13 years.) Baseball is in our blood. Whenever we get Yankees tickets, we always arrive when the gates open, hours before the game, to take in batting practice; you might also snag player autographs if you arrive early.

Another reason to get to the stadium way before the first pitch is to rub Babe Ruth's head in Monument Park (Roger Clemens rubbed his head before each pitching outing he had). Before each game, they line up to visit Monument Park, but it moves quickly, so don't be put off by the crowd.

If the Yanks aren't in town or you don't want or can't go to a game, you can still take a tour to see the famous stadium. Bonus: The tours are given year-round. The Classic Tour includes field access, and visits to the dugout, the press box, Monument Park and the Clubhouse. Cost: Adults $12 ($14 in June, July and August), kids (14 years old and under) $6 ($7 in June, July and August), and senior citizens (60 years old and older) $6 ($7 in June, July and August). There are two other tours that, in addition to the above, include things like a movie about the Yankees history, but these tours are limited to groups. You can buy tickets online for the tour, but you must do so at least 10 days in advance, otherwise purchase your tickets at the Stadium's Advance Ticket

Windows. There are other restrictions, such as no tours on game days. Check the website for more specifics and updated information.

Note: Tickets to games are expensive and prohibitive for some families. Good news: There are certain games with discounted ticket prices. Check the webite for updated info. The Bleacher seats are the cheapest but there's another price to pay—the bleacher creatures: a rowdy (although good-natured) crowd. If you've got young kids and are concerned about raucous seatmates, reserve seats in the alcohol free section. But security at the stadium is tight and the crowd generally behaves.

A great New York moment: The minute the game ends, win or lose, the classic song *New York, New York* is blasted throughout the speakers—several times while the mass exodus of baseball fans occurs. Note: Frank Sinatra's version of New York is played if the Yankees win; if they lose it's someone else (shame on me for not knowing; hopefully they'll win if you take in a game so you won't know what I'm talking about). We always stay put in our seats to soak it all in (no matter if they've won or lost) for as long as we can—eventually we're asked to leave. As you can imagine, the subway platforms are packed, so what's the rush? Savor the moment.

Parent Tip

You can buy hot dogs and other standard stadium fare like fries, soda, chicken sandwiches and pizza in Yankee Stadium—but it'll cost you practically as much as the ticket to get in. And, thanks to tight security, you are not allowed to bring in cans, bottles and huge picnic spreads. Still, baseball without a hot dog is practically sacreligious. Time to compromise. There's a hot dog vendor just outside the stadium (by the giant baseball bat) who sells good dogs and the prices are lower.

There's also a bowling place across the street that we frequent before games start. Mind you, we've never bowled here. But we have used the bathrooms often. (If you arrive at the Stadium very early like we do to beat the traffic and to catch batting practice the gates are sometimes still closed and you cannot enter the Stadium. That's when the bowling alley becomes handy).

The Bronx Zoo/Wildlife Conservation Park

Bronx River Parkway and Fordham Road, 718/367-1010, www.bronxzoo.com.
Open: Monday through Friday 10am to 5pm, Saturday and Sunday 10am to 5:30pm.

Admission: $11 adults, $8 seniors/students and kids, kids under 2 are free. Note: Wednesday is pay-what-you-wish day.

Subways: 2, 5.

If you're zoo lovers, you'll flip for this animal kingdom. It's the largest urban zoo in the United States (265 acres) and is home to thousands of animals, birds, fish and reptiles. The Bronx Children's Zoo, a zoo within a zoo, is a big hit with kids who can pet domesticated animals and ride camels. The sea lion and penguin feedings are also big hits. The Congo Gorilla Forest is another popular attraction. My son loves the tram and monorail rides that crisscross the zoo.

One of the most exciting adventures in town is at the Family Overnight Safari here. You get to spend the night in a tent at the zoo. The safari is offered three times a year between the months of May through September. To register, go to www.bronxzoo.com/bz-education; the program fills up fast so it's wise to book way ahead. Cost: $250 for adult/child pair. (Central Park Zoo offers a similar program; see separate listing).

Cloisters Museum
99 Margaret Corbin Drive, Fort Tryon Park, 212/923-3700, www.metmuseum.org.

Open: Tuesday through Sunday 9:30am to 5:15pm; November through February closing time is 4:45pm.

Admission: $12 adults, $7 seniors.

Open: November through February, Tuesday through Sunday 9:30am to 5pm March through October, Tuesday through Sunday 9:30am to 5:30pm Closed Thanksgiving, Christmas and New Year's Day.

Subway: A to 190th Street, then M4 bus to Fort Tyron Park-The Cloisters stop.

A branch of the Metropolitan Museum of Art is one indication that this gem is classy and top notch. The Cloisters sits pretty in a four-acre setting on a hilltop peering over the Hudson River in Fort Tryon Park. The setting is one reason to visit. There are others: It's the only museum in America devoted exclusively to medieval art. And the Unicorn tapestries are really cool. Technically it's located on Manhattan's northernmost tip, but I'm including it in the Bronx section, because it's a schlep from Manhattan's main tourist zones and it's practically in the Bronx.

Wave Hill
675 West 252nd Street (at Independence Avenue), Bronx, 718/549-3200, www.wavehill.org.

Train: MetroNorth to Riverdale station.

Open: Tuesday through Sunday 9am to 4:30pm. From mid-May to mid-October open until 5:30pm, and June through August open on Wednesday until 9pm. Closed Monday.

Admission: Free on Saturday mornings, all day Tuesday and mid-November through mid-March. Otherwise, $4 adults, $2 students and seniors, free for kids ages 5 years and under .

A sprawling, 28-acre public garden with views of the Hudson River and the Palisades, woos families on sunny days. Let 'em loose: kids can roam the pretty gardens and lawn. Bonus: Weekend programs (1pm to 4pm) in horticultural and the arts for kids. Advance reservations are not required.

Edgar Allan Poe Cottage

East Kingsbridge and Grand Concourse, Bronx, 718/881-8900, www.bronxhistoricalsociety.org.

Call for times and admission.

If your children love poetry, they'll be interested in this restored home of Edgar Allan Poe, where he wrote *Annabel Lee,* among other poems. There's a film presentation and a guided tour.

Chapter 8

I'M HUNGRY!

New York City is home to some of the world's best chefs and most celebrated restaurants. The challenge, of course, is finding a restaurant that will appease all family members and will not compromise your budget. The good news is there are family-friendly spots where the food is agreeable to both parents and kids, as well as the ambience.

One of the most popular trends in family dining in the City is something called **PlayDine**, considered a godsend by many New York parents, and tourists too. PlayDine is the brainstorm of Dan Lowenstein, a dad of two young kids who became frustrated by the lack of family-friendly dining options in town. The way it works: you all sit down to eat as a family at the restaurant but, while the kids are waiting for their meal and after they've eaten, they can play in a supervised play center with "nannies" so that mom and dad can savor their meal in peace.

An admission fee is charged for each child (kids up to nine years old are eligible) who uses the activity center but kids can play for the duration of their parents' meal. The cost: $10 for one child, $9 per child for two children, $8 per child for three or more children. If you buy 10 admissions, the 11th one is free. Note: There is a food and drink minimum for each adult that has a child using PlayDine: $8 lunch and $12 dinner. Reservations are recommended. Note: Mom or dad and each child get matching invisible hand stamps for security. Also, all nannies have clean background checks and CPR training and are watched by a nannycam.

There are three restaurants in the City that offer PlayDine: **La Belle Epoque** in Greenwich Village, **Big City Bar and Grill** on the Upper East Side and **Sambuca** on the Upper West Side (see separate listings in the restaurant section).

As this book went to press, PlayDine had plans to expand the concept into other restaurants; for up-to-date information, visit www.playdine.com or call 212/866-6585.

And if you're a foodie (like Iam), and the key to a great vacation for your family is eating well, consider planning your visit to New York during one of the city's **Restaurant Weeks**—typically held in late January or early February and then again in June. The way it works: More than 200 restaurants throughout the city offer a set price for lunch and dinner. The best part: The lineup includes the most sought after, priciest restaurants in town. For more info, call or visit www.nycvisit.com

LOWER MANHATTAN
McDonald's
160 Broadway, 212/385-2063.

$.

Yep, it's a McDonald's, but there' a white gloved doorman and a piano player at this Mickey D's in the Financial District. Afterall, powerful stockbrokers and City Hall government officials chow down on Big Macs at this Golden Arches. Kids, of course, get a kick out of the fanciness of it all.

Parent Tip
When visiting the Big Apple the temptation is strong to stop for a quick and cheap meal at one of New York's hot dog and knish vendors. They're everywhere. But, if you're in the Wall Street area, do like the movers and shakers: head for the **Daisy May's BBQ USA** cart parked in the vicinity of 40 Wall Street for a cup of gourmet chili that'll have you swear you're in the Lone Star State. The chef, Adam Perry Lang, is a Daniel Boulud-trained chef (translation: excellent pedigree). The chili is served with homemade hot sauce and a flour tortilla, and you can order a side dish of beans. Cost: $6 for a 12-ounce cup.

Bonus: There are two additional Daisy May carts in midtown at Broadway and 39th Street and at Sixth Avenue and 50th Street. To enjoy your chili while sitting outside in a small park with a waterfall and a piece of the Berlin Wall in it (yep, the Berlin Wall), walk a couple of blocks to 53rd Street just off Fifth Avenue, on the north side across the street from the Harper Collins Building.

LITTLE ITALY & CHINATOWN

Little Italy

Umberto's Clam House

178 Mulberry Street (corner of Broome Street), 212/431-7545, www.umbertosclamhouse.com.

Open: Daily 11am to 4pm.

$$.

Clams (baked, littleneck, cherrystones) are only half the story at this popular Italian restaurant specializing in Italian seafood specialties. Umberto's has been on the scene in Little Italy way before *The Sopranos* made it big.

Casa Bella Ristorante Bar-Cafe

127 Mulberry Street (between Hester and Canal streets), 212/431-4080, www.casabellarestaurant.com.

$$.

Open: Sunday through Thursday noon to midnight, Friday and Saturday noon to 1am.

Mangia here May through October and you're in for a real treat when the outdoor café is open. No matter what time of year you visit though, the food is what you'd expect from a popular Italian restaurant in Little Italy with a traditional menu: antipasto, spaghetti, manicotti, tortellini, fetuccine, ravioli with delicious sauces, as well as hearty meat and seafood dishes.

Lombardi's

32 Spring Street (between Mott and Mulberry Streets), 212/941-7994.

Monday through Thursday 11:30am to 11pm, Friday and Saturday 11:30am to midnight, Sunday 11:30am to 10pm.

$.

Practically since the beginning of time, this popular Little Italy pizza joint has been rolling out and rolling in the dough. You want a good New York pizza pie? You come here.

Chinatown

Chinatown is spot-on for dim sum, the Cantonese term for small dishes meaning "a little bit of heart." There are hundreds of types of steamed and fried dim sum (meat, vegetarian, fish). Usually you select from carts that are pushed throughout a dim sum restaurant.

Jing Fong

20 Elizabeth Street (between Canal and Bayard streets), 212/964-5256.

Open: Monday through Friday 10:30am to 3:30pm and 5pm to 11pm, Saturday and Sunday 9am to 3:30pm and 5pm to 11pm.

$$.

A hugely popular Chinatown restaurant in an equally large space—eating here is an event, not just a meal. You must experience dim sum here—carts with more than 100 dim sum items are whizzed around the room by the hi-tech waitstaff who wear microphone headsets. You'll see lots of Chinese families dining at this festive restaurant.

Golden Unicorn

18 East Broadway (at Catherine Street). 212/941-0911.
Open: Monday through Friday 9am to 11pm, Saturday and Sunday 8am to 11pm, dim sum is served daily between 9am and 3:30am.
$$.
Another very popular Chinatown dim sum hot spot—the selection is enormous and so is the dining space.

Triple Eight Palace

88 East Broadway (between Division and Market streets), 212/941-8886.
$$.
Yep, dim sum is the name of the game at this popular restaurant, too.

New York Noodletown

28 1/2 Bowery (at Bayard St.), 212/349-0923.
Open: Monday through Sunday 9am to 4am.
$$.
You won't find dim sum here, but if your kids love noodles this is a good choice. Think noodle soup, pan fried noodles, lo mein. The restaurant is also known for its salt baked shrimp.

Chinatown Ice Cream Factory

65 Bayard Street (between Mott and Elizabeth streets), 212/608-4170.
Open: Monday through Friday 11am to 10:30pm, Saturday and Sunday 11am to 11pm.
Not your traditional ice cream flavors (green tea, taro and lychee), but there's vanilla, too.

SOHO/TRIBECA/GREENWICH VILLAGE/EAST VILLAGE
Balthazar

80 Spring Street (between Crosby and Broadway streets), 212/965-1785, www.balthazarny.com.
Open: Breakfast Monday through Friday 7:30am to 11:30pm, Saturday and Sunday 8am to 10am; lunch Monday through Friday noon to 3pm; late lunch Monday through Friday 3pm to 5pm; dinner Monday through Saturday 5:45pm to midnight, Sunday 5:30pm to 11pm; after hours Monday through

Thursday midnight to 1am, Friday and Saturday midnight to 2am, Sunday 11pm to midnight.

$$$.

This French bistro-style restaurant with its red leather banquettes, smoky mirrors and *joie de vivre* mood is one of my favorite places to eat in the city. And I'm not alone; this is one of the most popular restaurants in town. Come for breakfast and your kids will love the Nutella on a baguette. Your kids will also adore the *steak frites* (french fries), believe by many food critics to be the best in town. The raw bar at Balthazar is incredible; 75 types of oysters. Balthazar is open until the wee hours of the morning—fun if you've got older teens that want to go somewhere hip after a Broadway show or Yankee or Met game, for instance. Tables are close together—you may rub elbows (figuratively and literally) with New York celebs. *C'est la vie* in the Big City.

Note: You will be hugely disappointed, as we were recently, if you don't make reservations and expect to be seated during peak times (translation: most of the day). I had raved about this place to my mom and one weekend afternoon came here to dine. The wait list was over two hours. One day, mom, I promise!

Zoe

90 Prince Street (between Broadway and Mercer streets), 212/966-6722, www.zoerestaurant.com.

Open: Lunch Tuesday through Friday noon to 3pm; dinner Tuesday through Thursday 6pm to 10:30pm, Friday 6pm to 11pm, Saturday 5:30pm to 11:30pm, Sunday 5:30pm to 10pm; brunch Saturday and Sunday 11:30am to 3pm.

$$.

We settled into a booth in this pleasant restaurant, nibbled over food we'd ordered from the American-cuisine-inspired menu, and lingered for hours. There are also tables, but there is something about a booth that's almost like a high chair—my son is a captive audience when he's in a booth even though he's 13 years old (especially if we make him scoot to the inside by the wall!).

The open kitchen with a wood burning oven, grill and rotisserie brings everyone together—especially kids who can opt to order off the Kid's Dinner Menu and have the restaurant's culinary team explain to them the cooking process. The non-traditional kids' menu includes fun, experimental things like: Zoe's famous crispy calamari and dipping sauce ($5.50), and main plates that include everything from pasta to sliced steak to free-range chicken breast. There's even a special children's house cocktail: the Pineapple Surprise.

Broome Street Bar

363 West Broadway, www.broomestreetbar.com, 212/925-2086.

Open: Sunday through Thursday 11am to 1:30am, Friday and Saturday 11am to 2:30am, Saturday and Sunday 11am to 4pm.

$.

A favorite haunt of locals (you almost expect Norm from *Cheers* to swing through the doors), you can't miss at this Soho institution (it's been here more than 30 years) with its comforting neighborhood ambience. When I lived down the street I'd hang here often. Think burgers ($6.50 and up), sandwiches like a tuna melt ($7) and creative salads ($8.50). Broome Street also serves a popular brunch on Saturday and Sunday between 11am and 4pm.

The Odeon

145 West Broadway (between Duane and Thomas streets), 212/233-0507, www.theodeonrestaurant.com.

Open: Monday through Friday noon to 1:30am, Saturday and Sunday 11:30am to 1:30am.

$$$.

If you've got sophisticated kids and want to experience a trendy and legendary New York restaurant, this is a great spot. Once *the* place to eat, Odeon is yesterday's news but still popular with nostalgic New Yorkers and celebs. Old standbys like chicken and burgers round out the menu that also features bistro-type delicacies like pate.

Bubby's

120 Hudson Street (at North Moore Street), 212/219-0666.

Open: Breakfast, lunch and dinner daily.

$.

Buttermilk pancakes, potato pancakes, meatloaf, fried chicken and incredible pies all served in a we-are-family atmosphere.

Pearl Oyster Bar

18 Cornelia Street (between Bleeker and West 9th streets), 212/691-8211, www.pearloysterbar.com.

Open: For lunch, Monday through Friday noon to 2:30pm; and for dinner Monday through Saturday 6pm to 11pm.

$$.

Oddly, there aren't *that* many seafood restaurants in this city, despite the fact that it's an island surrounded by water and the Atlantic Ocean is a subway ride away. Pearl Oyster Bar is one of only a handful of great seafood spots in Manhattan—lobster and oyster rolls, mussels in a mustard and wine cream sauce are specialties. It's tiny (even though it's recently expanded) and you'll wait for a table (reservations are not accepted) but if it's great seafood you crave with a cool Greenwich Village vibe, it's worth your while.

Burrito Bar

305 Church Street, 212/219-9200, www.burritobar.com.
Open: Sunday through Thursday 11:30am to 12am, Friday and Saturday 11:30am to 2am.
$.

Before you even step into the restaurant you'll find your first clue that it's kid-friendly; there's a gigantic purple bus amidst clouds hanging over the front door. Clue number two: Enter the restaurant and you'll step back into the '60s with fake Zebra skin covered waterbed sofas. You have to smile. The Children's Menu not only talks to the kids but to parents with its easy-on-the-wallet prices (the most expensive item on the children's menu is $3.95).

John's Pizzeria

278 Bleeker Street, 212/243-1680.
Open: Monday through Saturday 11:30am to 11:30pm, Sunday 11:30pm to 9pm.
$.

I've been inhaling pepperoni slices at this way-popular pizza joint way before my 13-year-old son was born, and it's just as popular now as it was then. You can't order individual slices but you won't want to—it's so good you'll devour an entire pie. Order it plain or select from the more than a dozen toppings. This is the original John's Pizzeria and it's got a lived-in-look, but locals wouldn't want it any other way. A second location, at Times Square, is equally popular but glossier. The Times Square restaurant is located at 260 West 44th Street.

Peanut Butter & Co.

240 Sullivan Street, www.ilovepeanutbutter.com.
Open: Sunday through Thursday 11am to 9pm, Friday and Saturday 11am to 10pm.
$.

The nuttiest of sandwiches are featured on the menu here. Think: "Peanut Butter Cup," freshly ground peanut butter, kissed with a layer of Nutella. Or, "The Heat Is On Sandwich," spicy peanut butter and chilled chicken, with a bit of pineapple jam. Or, the "White Chocolate Wonderful Sandwich," white chocolate peanut butter and orange marmalade. The menu also features non-peanut butter items, including tuna fish, turkey, and grilled cheese sandwiches. The shop is on quiet Sullivan Street, an off-the-beaten-path Soho street and there are benches out front where you can munch.

Katz's Deli

205 East Houston Street (at Ludlow Street), 212/254-2246, www.katzdeli.com.
$.

New York's oldest deli (it dates to the late 1800's) where the pastrami and corned beef sandwiches keep 'em lined up. The hot dogs are good, too. This is a quintessential Lower East Side New York deli.

Two Boots

37 Avenue A, 212/505-2276, www.twoboots.com.

Open: Sunday through Thursday 5pm to 11pm, Friday and Saturday 5pm to midnight, Saturday and Sunday brunch noon to 5pm.

First, the name: the boots represent the geographical shapes of Italy and Louisiana. The menu: Inspired by the cuisines of both those spots.

I had a strange introduction to this hugely popular restaurant (the first of many Two Boots located throughout the city). The first time I ate here I witnessed a rooftop chase across the street that ended tragically with the guy who was being chased falling off the roof and onto the sidewalk below.

Anyway...the food is fun and spicy and the ambience is fun-loving. Kids love the pizza—with all kinds of toppings, including the standard pepperoni to the more experiemental tasso (Cajun ham) and BB@ shrimp. Sandwiches are also on the menu like blackened catfish Po' Boy and eggplant parmigiana.

Other Two Boots locations: Two Boots Pizzeria at 42 Avenue A; Two Boots Grand Central (in the lower level dining concourse); Two Boots to Go-Go at 74 Bleeker Street in the Village; Two Boots to Go West at 201 West 11th Street; Two Boots Rock Center at Rockefeller Center (in the lower level dining concourse). There are also several Two Boots theaters, which offer cult films in retro settings but these aren't necessarily family-friendly.

The Original New York Milkshake Company

37 St. Marks Place (at Second Avenue), 212/505-5200.

Open: Sunday through Thursday 11:30am to midnight, Friday and Saturday 11:30am to 3am.

$.

Growing up, all of my baby teeth were extracted because the roots never dissolved. This involved many visits to the dentist to have one or two yanked at a time, a much-dreaded routine that seemed to go on for years. What is the relevance of this story to this restaurant? Well, the one "food" that I could easily negotiate during that time period following the extractions was a milkshake. It was a meal for me—breakfast, lunch and dinner. Thankfully, my son's roots dissolved and his baby teeth all fell out naturally. However, he liked my milkshake story so much, we have milkshake-for-dinner nights every so often. The delicious milkshakes here are meal-worthy (yet, they also have a limited menu including grilled cheese sandwiches).

La Belle Epoque

827 Broadway (between 12th and 13th streets), 646/382-6479. Playdine hours: Thursday, Friday and Saturday 11:30am to 8pm.

$$$.

Oui, oui, this is an elegant French Quarter-style restaurant in Greenwich Village, with the kind of food and ambience your kids will hate. And why is it included in a family travel guidebook? Enter: Playdine, a supervised restaurant-based play and babysitting center that's located right in the restaurant (see sidebar for more information about Playdine). The menu is a combo of Creole, French and Contemporary American. The mood is grown-up. The PlayDine concept is brilliant.

Silver Spurs Diner

490 LaGuardia Place (corner of Houston street), 212/228-BEEF.

Open: 7am.

$.

Giddyap to this popular neighborhood diner and order up a stack of pancakes or a turkey burger off the cutesy menu. Silver Spurs is the kind of place where the locals have been going forever, as well as in-the-know out-of-towners.

UNION SQUARE

Chat 'n' Chew

10 East 16th Street (between Fifth Avenue and Union Square West, 212/243-1616, www.chatnchewnyc.com.

Open: Lunch and dinner.

$$.

Down-home cooking in a farmhouse inspired setting appeal to families looking for a good comfort food meal. Uncle Red's Addiction, honey-dipped fried chicken, and killer macaroni and cheese keep everyone happy. Bonus: Free soda refills also keep the kids happy (maybe not the adults, though). Really yummy desserts, too.

CHELSEA

America

9 East 18th Street (Fifth Avenue), 212/505-2110, www.arkrestaurants.com.

Open: Saturday and Sunday noon to 4pm.

$.

Perfect for kids of all ages, thanks to the huge loft-like space, loud chatter, and longer-than-the-*Consitution*-menu. Each item is named for a town and state and includes tons of kid-friendly food. For instance, there's the $4.95 Fluffernutter sandwich (which the menu associates with Las Vegas, Nevada).

I love the salads here. Bonus: Come for Sunday brunch when a balloon artist and magician entertain the kids. Also, between 1pm and 3pm on Sundays, it's storytime for kids. The restaurant's Flatiron District location is a short walk to Madison Square Park, one of the best playgrounds for kids in the City.

Pastis

9 Ninth Avenue (corner of Little West 12th Street), 212/929-4844, www.pastisny.com.

Open: Breakfast 9am to noon daily; lunch noon to 6pm Monday through Friday; brunch noon to 5pm Saturday and Sunday; dinner 6pm to midnight daily; supper midnight to 2am Sunday through Thursday and midnight to 2:30am Friday and Saturday.

$$.

In the heart of the trendy Meatpacking District, this incredibly popular brasserie is celeb central. Owned by the same owners as Balthazar (see separate listing), Pastis is a treat—and is especially popular with Europeans living in or visiting the City. There are always kids in high chairs when we come here. Provencal cuisine is the thrust of the menu, but there kid-friendly items. Bonus: The bathroom is cool—there are separate men and women's toilets but you'll eventually met at the shared trough-like sink. Guaranteed for kid giggles.

Empire Diner

210 10th Avenue (at West 22nd Street), 212/243-2736.

Open: Daily 24 hours (except on Tuesdays between 4am and 8am).

$$.

When this diner in an old rail car first opened decades ago, it was a magnet for celebrities. Today, it still has a force, thanks to its outdoor seating and show tunes. The food isn't standard diner fare—in fact, don't come here for pancakes (they aren't on the menu, to many people's chagrin). Empire is a pretentious diner with a menu that's more akin to a nice restaurant than a New York City diner.

THEATER DISTRICT/TIMES SQUARE

ESPN Zone

1472 Broadway, 212/921-ESPN, www.espnzone.com.

Open: Sunday 11am to 11pm, Monday through Thursday 11:30am to 11pm, Friday 11:30am to midnight, Saturday 11am to midnight.

$$.

Sports lovers will score big at this thick-in-the-action Times Square hot spot. The kid's menu offers sports-themed items such as "sliders" or two mini cheeseburgers.

Café Edison

228 West 47th Street (in the Hotel Edison), 212/354-0368.
Open: Monday through Saturday 6am to 9:30pm, Sunday 6am to 7:30pm.
$.
A venerable New York hangout, with actors, producers, magicians who gather to talk shop, swap opening night stories and dine on homemade soups (matzo ball, borscht), sandwiches and burgers. Great spot to grab a bite to eat before the theater.

Planet Hollywood Times Square Restaurant & Bar

1540 Broadway (at 45th Street), 212/333-STAR, www.planethollywood.com.
Open: Lunch and dinner daily.
$$.
Ribs, burgers, movie memorabilia and movie displays, this popular tourist spot moved from its midtown location to Times Square. Founders Demi Moore, Arnold Schwarzenegger, Sylvester Stallone and Bruce Willis expanded this concept all over the country, so chances are you're already familiar with the theme and concept. There's a standard kid's menu of macaroni and cheese and other items that are not alien to youngsters.

Red Lobster

5 Times Square, 212/730-6706, www.redlobster.com.
Open: Lunch 11am, dinner 4pm.
$$$.
Chances are you're way familiar with this seafood chain—but this is the glitziest of them all. The Times Square restaurant spans three-levels and has in a short time become one of the most popular spots to dine in Times Square. Two, 420-gallon aquariums and a revolving, 10-foot tall neon-lit lobster splash things up a couple of notches. They line up to get in. I feel compelled to include this chain restaurant because it is family-friendly. However, it goes without saying, in a city like New York, with a gazillion restaurants, Red Lobster probably isn't high on your list.

Ruby Foo's

1626 Broadway (at 49th Street), 212/489-5600, www.brquestrestaruants.com.
Open: Sunday through Wednesday 11:30am to midnight, Thursday through Saturday 11:30am to 1am.
$$$.
This three-level, upbeat pan-Asian restaurant is a crowd-pleaser with its Japanese, Chinese, Thai menu and spirited atmosphere. Thanks to its Times Square location and eye-bulging Asian-inspired décor, this eatery gets busy; reservations are recommended. Bonus: Crayons and coloring books for

impatient youngsters. There is second Ruby Foo's location uptown at 2182 Broadway (at 77th Street), 212/724-6700.

Virgil's BBQ

152 West 44th Street (between 6th and Broadway), 212/921-9494, www.virgilsbbq.com.

Open: Sunday through Monday 11:30am to 11pm, Tuesday through Saturday 11:30am to midnight.

$$.

Owned by the same folks who own the incredibly successful Carmine's italian restaurants, Virgil's steals hearts of those who have a hankering for great barbecue. The menu features hard-core, finger-lickin' barbecue like Memphis pork ribs, Owensboro lamb, Maryland smoked ham, biscuits, cornbread, grits and barbecue beans. Save room for the pecan pie. Smack those lips.

Manhattan Chili Company

1500 Broadway (entrance on 43rd Street), 212/730-8666 www.manhattanchili.com.

Open: Daily 11:30am to midnight.

$$.

A Southwestern-inspired restaurant that's conveniently located in spicy Times Square, there's (of course) chili on the menu (a kid pleaser) with many toppings choices. But there are also fun items like coconut shrimp tacos, grilled chicken with guacamole wraps and burgers.

Carmine's

200 West 44th Street (between 7th and 8th avenues), 212/221-3800, www.carminesnyc.com.

Open: Sunday 11am to 11pm, Monday 11:30am to 11pm, Tuesday 11:30am to 11pm, Wednesday 11am to midnight, Thursday through Saturday 11:30am to midnight.

$$.

Southern Italian food served family-style (big platters) in a lively, festive setting. Any Italian dish you can dream up is on the menu. Promise. A feel-good, kind of place that families love. *Pass the veal parm please*. Note: There's another Carmine's on the Upper West Side at 2450 Broadway (between 90th and 91st street), 212/362-2200; open Sunday through Thursday 11:30am to 11pm and Friday and Saturday 11:30 to midnight.

MIDTOWN
Cupcake Café
522 9ᵗʰ Avenue (at 39ᵗʰ Street, behind Port Authority), 212/465-1530, www.cupcakecafe.com.

Open: Monday through Friday 7am to 7pm, Saturday 8am to 7pm, Sunday 9am to 5pm.

$.

The icing on the cake at this eatery in the neighborhood known as Hell's Kitchen is quite literally the icing on the cake. You'll want to make the trip here just for the buttercream frosted cupcakes. Yes, you can order from a limited menu (soups and pasta), but it's the iced cupcakes that'll rope you in.

Jekyll and Hyde
1409 Avenue of the Americas, 212/541-9505, www.eerie.com.

Open: Monday through Thursday 11:30am to midnight, Friday 11:30am to 1am, Saturday 10:30 to 1am, Sunday 11am to midnight.

$$.

We celebrated my son's 8ᵗʰ birthday in this kooky restaurant and Alex loved it. It's a theme restaurant, so expect lots of Jekyll and Hyde-inspired fun. The menu's predictable though, with whimsically named items like The Mummy—"sirloin bandaged in your choice of cheese." The kid's menu (10 and younger) features pizza, chicken finger, PBJ and pasta. There are also offerings of yellow fin tuna and rib eye steak for hungry adults. Kids adore this place,

Parent Tip
Burger Heaven, a small chain of diner-like restaurants in midtown, is a good spot for families on the go. Around the corner from my old office, there is a Burger Heaven (536 Madison Avenue between 53ʳᵈ and 54ᵗʰ streets; 212/753-4214) where I used to eat breakfast or lunch—most often when my son came to the office with me. The food is consistently good, the service is fast (these restaurants cater to the business crowd, as well as tourists) and the place is clean. Burgers, salads, sandwiches, milkshakes, you name it, Burger Heaven's got it. They serve breakfast, too.

Bonus: The **Sony Technology Wonder Lab** is just around the corner. A smaller Burger Heaven is a block away at 9 East 53ʳᵈ Street; 212/755-2166. There are also three additional midtown locations: 20 East 49ᵗʰ Street, 212/755-2198; 804 Lexington Avenue at 62ⁿᵈ Street, 212/838-3580; and 291 Madison Avenue at 41ˢᵗ Street, 212/685-6250.

but note that it can be a scary experience for toddlers and infants. There's a Greenwich Village sidekick but it's much smaller and not nearly as good.

Ellen's Stardust Diner
1659 Broadway (at 51st Street), 212/956-5151, www.ellensstardustdiner.com.
Open: Monday through Thursday 7am to midnight, Friday through Saturday 7am to 1am, Sunday 7am to 1am.
$$.
The singing waitstaff is one of the lures of this retro 1950's-themed diner (you can't miss it, its exterior is dolled up in bright red and blue). Other treats: an indoor choo-choo that snakes around the eatery's mezzanine, videos from 1950's shows, and a fun menu of typical diner stuff, including blue plate specials (turkey, chicken pot pie), hot dogs, deli sandwiches, grilled cheese. Our neighbor, 8-year-old Mary Peirce insists this is her favorite restaurant in NYC and she especially loves the pizza here. A kid's menu ($7.50) has standard stuff like burgers and chicken fingers.

Carnegie Deli
854 Seventh Avenue (at West 55th Street), 212/757-2245, www.carnegiedeli.com.
Open until 4am.
$.
Home of the pastrami, Carnegie Deli is a celebrity—and tourist favorite. A bowl of crunchy dill pickles is as standard a tabletop item as the forks and knives. Matzoh ball soup and other Jewish mother specialties are also popular here.

Serendipity
225 East 60th Street (between 2nd and 3rd avenues), 212/838-3531, www.serendipity3.com.
Open: Sunday through Thursday 11:30am to midnight, Friday 11:30am to 1am, Saturday 11:30am to 2am.
$$.
*Frrrr*ozen hot chocolate ($6.50) is what put this restaurant on the map as a must-experience place for kids to try—especially kids of celebs who come here on a regular basis to celebrate birthdays. Sit upstairs or downstairs. There's also a menu of soups, salads, omelets, burgers, foot long hot dogs...but it's the *frrrr*ozen hot chocolate that keeps 'em coming back.

Mickey Mantle's Restaurant
42 Central Park South, 212/688-7777, www.mickeymantles.com.
$$.
This is my son's favorite New York City restaurant. It's got a great buzz about it even if you're not a baseball nut like he is. There's a lively bar in front,

with the requisite television sets to watch live sports events—baseball in the summer, of course. You can also buy authentic autographed baseballs, bats and T-shirts, and other memorabilia (pricey, though). In the back there's a multi-level dining room, again with television sets strategically located. We always snag a booth and settle in for ribs and burgers. There's also the Spring Training Menu, a healthy, low fat, low-calories menu, from which my son's dad always orders (grilled fish, pasta). The Little League Menu is for kids 12 years and under and offers usual kid fare like chicken fingers, macaroni and cheese, pasta with tomato sauce, grilled cheese and burgers with waffle fries; every item is $8.95 and comes with a Mickey Mantle souvenir. Another thing this casual restaurant has going for it—its' location across the street from Central Park.

Mars 2112 Restaurant and Bar

1633 Broadway (at 51st Street), 212/582-2112, www.mars2112.com.
Open: Monday through Thursday noon to 9pm, Friday noon to midnight, Saturday 11:30am to midnight, Sunday 11:30am to 9pm.
$$.
A theme attraction cum restaurant with an alien spaceship hanging over the entrance, kids will beg you to eat here. Be prepared for an outer body experience when you receive the bill; prices are out of this world for standard fare of burgers and chicken (not unlike the other theme restaurants in town) but Mars 2112 won't disappoint the kids. Captain Orion entertains.

The Palm Court at the Plaza Hotel

768 Fifth Avenue (59th Street), 212/759-3000, www.fairmont.com.
Afternoon tea: Monday through Saturday 3:45pm to 6pm, Sunday 4pm to 6pm.
$$.
Come here for tea with your Eloise-wannabe! Visitors come to The Plaza for a quintessential afternoon tea experience. The Children's Afternoon Tea is priced at $19.50 per person and includes Nutella and bananas, PBJ and ham and cheese sandwiches, as well as scones with Devonshire cream and preserves, pastries and choice of aromatic tea, hot cocoa, ice tea or milk. Pinky up! There are other afternoon teas available, including a Traditional tea and a Champagne Tea (glass of champagne is also served). Note: No shorts or sandals; jeans and sneakers "are tolerated." Men must wear slacks and collared shirts. (No reservations: first come, first served unless party of more than eight.)

The Waldorf Astoria

301 Park Ave. (between 49and 50th streets), 212/872-4818, www.nycwa-restaurant_reservations@hilton.com.

Afternoon tea: Tuesday through Saturday 3pm to 5:15pm. $$.

Come here for tea with your princess or prince. It's a treat to sip tea and munch on delicate edibles at the Warldorf's Cocktail Terrace that overlooks the famous Art Deco lobby. Scones, finger sandwiches, pastries and, of course, tea are served.

Parent Tip

I'm always searching for "adult" spots in Manhattan where it's perfectly acceptable to sip a glass of wine or a cocktail while kids can slurp Shirley Temples and Roy Rogers or other non-alcoholic drinks in a grown-up setting, aka cocktail lounge. I love the "Living Room" lounge at the **W New York Hotel**, on Lexington Avenue, a low-key scene—grab the coveted couch in front of the fireplace (on a winter's day). There are lots of living room-type chairs, as well as chessboards. There's also a reasonably priced snack menu—the fruit and cheese platter is really good. It's adult enough for me, without compromising Alex's innocence.

Another cool spot to sip and chat: at the lounge at the W Hotel in Times Square (47th and Broadway). A funky, red décor shouts out to teens that this is one hip place.

UPPER EAST SIDE
DT-UT

1626 2nd Avenue (between 84th and 85th Streets), 212/327-1327, www.dtut.com.

Open: Sunday through Thursday 8am to 12am, Friday and Saturday 8am to 2am.

$.

Cozy up to this quirky café where overstuffed vintage sofas and armchairs embrace diners of all ages. While you might slouch, the menu is no slouch—in fact, it's one of the most creative menus in the Big Apple, and knows what kids want. Here's a sampling; S'mores Waffle ($5.25), Tootsie Roll Rice Krispie Treat ($3.50), Caramel Fondue (with apples and marshmallows for dipping; $10.50). Yes, there are non-sweet items on the menu, including soups, sandwiches, quiche and pizza. Non-couch potatoes can sit in the skylight-lit atrium. Bonus: Story Time for kids on Tuesdays at 11am and Wednesdays at 1pm, complete with cookies and milk ($7 per child); best for kids ages 1 to 4 years old, but all are welcome. Note: There's also a downtown DT-UT at 41 Avenue B (between 3rd and 4th streets, 212/477-1021).

Big City Bar & Grill

1600 Third Avenue (at 90th Street), 212/369-0808, www.bigcitybarandgrill.com.
Open: PlayDine hours are Monday and Tuesday noon to 8pm, Wednesday through Saturday noon to 6pm.
$$.
Eureka! This hip Upper East Side eatery has a quick-order kids' menu so your children can eat first leaving you to dine in peace while they plan in the PlayDine activity center. The kid's menu is priced at $4.95 and kids can choose from fun foods such as popcorn shrimp, teriyaki steak tidbits or Big City piggies (pigs 'n blankets); there are also veggie items they can choose from.

Tony's DiNapoli

1606 2nd Avenue and 82nd Street (between 83rd and 84th streets), 212/861-8686.www.tonysdinapoli.com.
$$.
You'll know you've arrived when you spy the giant red awning from halfway down the street. This Italian restaurant dishes out family-style platters (translation: giant portions that everyone shares) of lobster fra diavolo , veal fricatta , chicken scarpiello, eggplant parmigiana, sausage and peppers... Note: There's also a Tony's DiNapoli in Times Square at 43rd Street (between 6th Avenue and Broadway); you can order individual meals at this location.

Jackson Hole

1270 Madison Avenue (at 91st Avenue), 212/427-2820, www.jacksonholeburgers.com.
Open: Monday through Sunday 10am to 1am.
$$.
It's real simple: Kids love Jackson Hole hamburgers. All kinds of toppings dress the seven-ounce burgers: the Eastsider is smeared with bacon, cheese, ham, mushrooms, tomatoes and fried onions; the Southwest burger is blanketed with guacamole and raw onion. Have it your way—bare or top heavy. Chicken sandwiches and salads also make a respectable showing at this beefy burger restaurant, as do blue plate specials (shrimp, steak.) And the prices are respectable: Hot dogs are $2.20. The scene is casual and there's sidewalk seating in nice weather. There are so many Jackson Hole's in the City, you'd swear you were in Wyoming. Other locations: 232 East 64th Street, 212/371-7187; 1611 Second Avenue, 212/737-8788; 1270 Madison Avenue, 212/427-2820.

Googies

1491 Second Avenue (at 78th Street), 212/717-1122.
$$.
Googies elicits giggles from young kids, thanks to its menu of burgers, meatloaf, milkshakes and orange creamsicles—and, fun-loving name and

boxcar setting. Actually, Googies menu has an Italian accent with entrees like spinach ricotta ravioli and a daily risotto. Whatever, it's revered by families on the Upper East Side.

HARLEM
Sylvia's
328 Lenox Avenue, 212/996-0660, www.sylviassoulfood.com.
Open: Monday through Saturday 7:30am to 10:30pm, Sunday 1pm to 7pm.
For excellent soul food and clap-your-hands gospel music, head way uptown to Sylvia's in Harlem. Sylvia Woods and her family opened this joint as a 35-seat restaurant in 1962, which blossomed into a popular Harlem restaurant which seats 450 people today. Praise the food: smothered chicken, grits, fried chicken, collard greens, and Sylvia's famous BBQ ribs. Yes, there's burgers and chicken for non-adventurous kid's (or adults) palettes; kids' Jackson and Sam Weaver love Sylvia's macaroni and cheese. The best day to visit: Sunday, for the gospel music brunch that sets a contagious life-is-good mood.

CENTRAL PARK
The Boathouse Restaurant
Central Park Lake (off East 72nd Street), 212/517-2233, www.centralparknyc.org.
Open: Monday through Friday noon to 3:45pm for lunch, 6pm to 10pm for dinner; Saturday and Sunday open 11am to 3:45pm for lunch, 6pm to 10pm for dinner. Closed for lunch November through March.
$$.
On a pretty day, we've eaten here outside and watched the boats sail on the Lake. New American cuisine and seafood grace the menu but it's not the food that wins a loyal clientele. It's the location on the lake. After or before your meal, you can rent canoes, rowboats or take a gondola ride.

Tavern on the Green
Central Park West (at 67th Street), 212/873-3200, www.tavernonthegreen.com.
Open: Lunch—Weekdays noon to 3pm and weekends from 11am. Dinner—Sunday through Thursday 5:30pm to 10:30pm; Friday and Saturday 5pm to 11:45pm; Saturday and Sunday brunch 10am. Pre-theater dinner Monday through Friday 5pm to 6:30pm.
$$$.
Crystal chandeliers and walls of mirrors tell part of the story, but you shouldn't think this New York landmark restaurant is off-limits because it's too ritzy. Built to house sheep in the 1870's, Tavern on the Green can seat 1,500 people in its six dining rooms. The restaurant is family-friendly—if you know

how to do it. From May to October you can eat al fresco in the garden or, come just for cocktails in the garden bar. The garden is the restaurant's best feature—at night the lights twinkle in the trees and, no matter what kind of day you've had in the City, you'll fall in love with Manhattan in this setting. Bonus: Order off the garden grill menu for lunch (Monday through Friday) or dinner (seven days a week). Or, come for the prix fixe pre-theater dinner at $32 a pop, Sunday through Thursday.

UPPER WEST SIDE
@SQC
270 Columbus Avenue (between 72nd and 73rd streets), 212/579-0100, www.sqcnyc.com.

Open: Monday through Friday 8am, Saturday, Sundays and holidays 9am.

Before or after your Central Park fling, whether it be a stroll or a frisbee catch, stop here for one of Chef Scott Q Campbell's (hence, the restaurant's name) famous beverages, such as peanut butter hot chocolate. The menu is fun, too. Breakfast items include fresh organic baby food, pumpkin-jam-filled pumpkin muffins, toasted sesame dusted donuts, omelets, and blueberry pancakes. Healthy sandwiches and salads round out the lunch menu, such as the roasted Roma tomatoes, fresh mozzarella and olive tapenade on rustic salami loaf. Dinner: chocolate BBQ spare ribs, grilled duck breast with confit and blackberries jus. Kids love the peppermint twist ice cream, and other flavors.

Gray's Papaya
2090 Broadway (at 71st Street), 212/799-0243, www.grayspapaya.com.
Open: 24/7.
$.

Well, let's put it this way: The food's not great but you gotta visit just once to buy a not-so-great hot dog and a cold papaya juice drink (does the job on a hot summer day). I've been coming here since the days right out of college when I lived in an illegal sublet on West 72nd street. But, boy, did we have fun scarfing down those dogs and papaya drinks at this open-24-hours New York institution. I wouldn't touch one of those dogs now (and you'll be skeptical, too) but your kids will love everything about this place. It's a rite of passage kind of thing.

EJ's Luncheonette
447 Amsterdam Avenue (between 81st and 82nd streets), 212/873-3444.
Open: Breakfast, lunch and dinner.
$.

My son and I lived just a couple of blocks away when this instantly-popular luncheonette opened more than 10 years ago and its been wowing kids and adults with egg creams and other comforting food ever since. It's a convenient location for families visiting the American Museum of Natural History and The Children's Museum of Manhattan. In the past decade, EJ's has since cloned and opened in two other locations—1271 Third Avenue, 212/472-0600 and 432 Sixth Avenue, 212/873-3444.

Dallas BBQ
27 West 72nd Street (off Central Park West), 212/873-2004.
Open: Sunday through Thursday 11am to 2am, Friday and Saturday 11am to 1am.
$$.
I've eaten many times here—before I had kids and with kids. It's one of the best values in town. Start off with a loaf of the famous onion rings (Spanish onions) and move on to the rotisserie BBQ chickens (no additives, no sauces, made every hour on hour). We usually order a quarter-chicken meal that comes with cornbread and choice of baked or fried Idaho potatoes. The cost: $3.95. Yep, $3.95. Oh, the drinks here are humongous—the strawberry dacquiris are the perfect complement to the zingy barbecued chicken.

Note: Dallas BBQ has spread its wings and opened up restaurants all over town. The locations: In the West Village at 21 University Place (near New York University and Washington Square Park; 212/674-4450); in the East Village at 132 Second Avenue (at St. Mark's Place; 212/777-5574); and in Chelsea at West 23rd Street (and 8th Avenue; 212/462-0001).

Popover Café
551 Amsterdam Avenue (at 86th Street), 212/595-8555, www.popover.com.
Open: Monday through Friday 8am to 10pm, Saturday and Sunday 9am to 10pm.
$$.
Cuddly teddy bears and fresh-from-the-oven popovers smeared with jam turn most kids on at this Upper West Side treasure—and their parents, too. I love the popovers here. Yes, the kids can hug the teddy bears that are all over the restaurant, and they can also draw portraits of the bears (or whatever they wish) with the crayons that they're given. Popovers are actually only the sidekick to a menu of sandwiches, soups and salads, and there's also a menu for children.

Sarabeth's
423 Amsterdam Avenue (at 80th Street), 212/496-6280, www.sarabeth.com.
Open: Monday through Saturday 8am to 11pm, Sunday 8am to 10pm.
$$.
Sarabeth and her husband opened Sarabeth's with the intention of selling her award-winning preserves and marmalade. Today, Sarabeth's is one of the

hottest tickets in town for brunch—when we lived down the block I'd marvel at the crowds of yuppified West Siders with their *New York Times*, lined up for hours to get a seat. They're still lining up. The rustic, sprig-of-forsythia-kind-of-country-setting is refreshing and the food is consistently good (waffles, omelets, pancakes and that marvelous jam and marmalade).

Sarabeth's popularity has taken the city by storm with two other locations. Sarabeth's (east) is located at 1295 Madison Avenue (at 92nd Street), 212/410-7335 and Sarabeth's at the Whitney Museum is located at 945 Madison Avenue (at 75th Street), 212/570-3670. Sarabeth's Bakery is located in the Chelsea Market at 75 Ninth Avenue (at 15th Street); 212/989-2424.

Parent Tip

One of my favorite restaurants in New York is **Café des Artistes**, a wonderful French restaurant not far from Central Park. (The owner, famed restaurateur George Lang just celebrated his 80th birthday.) Café des Artistes is an upscale restaurant and you should only come if you have older kids or very well behaved children. The walls are done up with artistic murals of nude women and the menu features things like *pot au feu*. We've sat at the bar over a drink, a nice treat if you suddenly find yourself without kiddies or your children are much older. There's also the Café des Artistes Parlor, a mini version of the restaurant, across the vestibule. Located at 1 West 67th Street, www.cafedesartistesnyc.com.

Alice's Tea Cup

102 West 73rd Street (at Columbus Avenue), 212/799-3006, www.alicesteacup.com.

Open: Tuesday through Friday, 11:30am to 8pm, Saturday 10:30am to 10pm and Sunday 11am to 8pm.

$.

A sweet spot for kids with a menu that has a healthy bent: pureed baby food, homemade graham crackers and Granny Smith apple slices with peanut butter or Nutella. This is also a great spot to experience afternoon tea for kids. The Wee Tea (for children under 10 years old) features scones, sandwiches and mousse.

Café con Leche

726 Amsterdam Avenue (between 95th and 96th streets), 212/678-7000, www.cafeconleche.com.

Open: Monday through Sunday 11 to 11; brunch Monday through Friday 11am to 4pm and Saturday and Sunday 10am to 4pm.

$.

Come for an authentic taste of Cuban and Dominican cuisine. Think *huevos rancheros,* Dominican fried chicken, paella, beef empanadas, *ropa vieja* (shredded beef) and *arroz con pollo* (chicken with rice.) Don't worry, if your kids are traditionalists, there are pancakes and French toast on the brunch menu. There's a second location at 424amsterdam Avenue (at West 80th street).

H&H Bagels

2239 Broadway (at 80th Street, this is the original location, 212/595-8003) and 639 West 46th Street, 212/595-8000, www.handhbagel.com.

Open: Both locations are open 24 hours a day, seven days a week.

$.

In a word: bagel. They crank them out at H&H and smother them with cream cheeses, cold cuts, Nova lox, the works. New Yorkers will line up for H & H bagels—and your family should join them. It's bad *juju* to visit New York without eating a bagel at least once during your stay. With kids, you'll be tempted to feed them bagels breakfast, lunch and dinner. They're easy, they're cheap and they can be filled with anything from cream cheese to turkey to chopped chicken liver. Bagels fly out of the bins here so there's a good chance your bagel will be hot from the oven.

Trattoria Sambuca

20 West 72nd Street (between Columbus Avenue and Central Park West), 212/787-5656, www.sambucanyc.com.

Open: PlayDine hours are Sunday 3pm to 8pm, Monday and Tuesday 5pm to 8pm.

$$.

This casual, family-style Italian restaurant (you know, giant heaps of Italian food served on platters for everyone at the table to share), also offers PlayDine (see sidebar). The kid's menu costs $10 and includes spaghetti and a big meatball, chicken fingers and pasta with tomato sauce, among other items. The adult menu has everything you'd expect from a Southern Italian-inspired restaurant from chicken parm to shrimp scampi. *Mangia!*

Rosa Mexicano

61 Columbus Avenue (at 62nd Street), 212/977-7700, www.rosamexicano.com.

Open: Lunch, Monday through Friday noon to 3pm, Saturday and Sunday 11:30am to 2:30pm; dinner, Sunday 4pm to 10pm, Monday 5pm to 10:30pm, Tuesday through Saturday 5pm to 11:30pm.

$$.

Across the street from Lincoln Center, this huge Mexican restaurant has incredibly fresh guacamole and a fun, festive atmosphere. I dream about the guacamole at Rosa Mexicano. On the east side is the original, much smaller

Rosa Mexicano; 1063 First Avenue (at 58th Street), 212/753-7407 (closed for lunch, open for dinner 5pm to 11:30pm daily).

Columbus Bakery
474 Columbus Avenue, 212/724-6880, www.arkrestaurants.com.
Open: breakfast, lunch and dinner.
$.
A great spot for families to grab a table and sticky buns, bagels, croissants or oatmeal and granola and to enjoy it while admiring passersby that stroll Columbus Avenue. Note: There's also a Columbus Bakery located at 957 1st Avenue, 212/421-0334.

Chapter 9

WHICH ONE IS MY ROOM?

The New York City hotel industry is booming. With 70,572 hotel rooms—and counting.

Families will find a selection of hotels, all price ranges, and some with kid-friendly amenities and packages. And new hotels in previously untouched neighborhoods will—or recently have—debuted.

Unlike many destinations, New York doesn't really experience a true off-season or peak season. Christmas time is busy and hotel rates reflect that, but generally speaking, tourism is a year-round affair in the Big Apple and hotel rates don't fluctuate all that much. During the week, New York hotels cater to business travelers—and the higher weekday rates are indicative of that. Weekend rates are usually lower; keep this in mind when booking. Also, always request a family rate or package. You can do so by calling the hotel's reservation desk directly.

Tip: The difference between a view of a parking lot and a view of the Empire State building is as significant as night and day. If you can afford it, splurge for a room with a view (yes, these rooms will cost more). A travel agent can tell you which of the hotel's rooms have views and which do not. Still, if you're stuck with the view of the dumpster in the hotel parking lot, it's not the end of the world. In New York, you won't spend much time in your room anyway.

Parking at hotel garages is exorbitantly high. Ouch! But many hotels throw in complimentary parking with weekend packages or other special promotions.

Keep in mind, a travel agent is your best bet because they are usually keyed into the most up-to-date rates and packages.

We've arranged the hotels by price categories and are based on per night, double occupancies. Keep in mind though, that all of these hotels offer packages—seasonal, family, weekend, or theme—and the rates vary considerably for each. Be sure to inquire about packages when making reservations.

Here are my price guidelines:
- **Very Expensive**: Over $200 ****
- **Expensive**: $150 to $200 ***
- **Moderate**: $100 to $150 **
- **Inexpensive**: Under $100 *

LOWER MANHATTAN
VERY EXPENSIVE ****
Ritz-Carlton New York, Battery Park

2 West Street, 800/241-3333 or 212/344-0800, www.ritzcarlton.com, 298 room and suites. Concierge. Health club and spa. Restaurant: Yes.

A 38-story waterfront hotel that is everything you'd expect from a Ritz-Carlton property—including the high-ticket price. The hotel has a great location—the ferries to Ellis Island and the Statue of Liberty are across the street and the New Skyscraper Museum is located in the same building as the hotel. The Ritz Kid's program puts on the Ritz, with a teddy-bear-tuck-in at turndown (say that ten times fast), a toy menu with games, G-rated movies and entertainment and get this, telescopes in the harborfront rooms for kids to spy on the lady across the way (The Statue of Liberty). Kids can order off a kid's menu which includes the Battery Park Pizza ($7) and the Skyscraper Burrito ($8).

EXPENSIVE ***
Millennium Hilton

55 Church Street, 800/445-8667 or 212/693-2001, www.hilton.com. 565 rooms. Restaurant: Yes. Concierge.

In the heart of the Financial District, this upscale property lived through 9/11 without any structural damage, and was restored and refurbished shortly after. It woos kids with its new indoor heated lap swimming pool in a new fitness center.

New York Marriott Financial Center Hotel

85 West Street. 800/242-8685 or 212/385-4900. www.marriottnyc.com. 500 rooms. Health club. Concierge. Restaurant: Yes.

Bingo: A swimming pool. Views of the Statue of Liberty is another draw, as well as affordable packages.

MODERATE **
Holiday Inn Wall Street
   15 Gold Street, 800/HOLIDAY or 212/232-7700, www.holidayinnwsd.com, 138 rooms. Concierge. Health club. Restaurant: Yes.
   This brand new hotel has a great downtown location for exploring interesting sites and attractions: the New York Stock Exchange, the Statue of Liberty, Ground Zero, South Street Seaport, and the museums of the American Indian and Jewish Heritage.

Best Western Seaport Inn
   33 Peck Slip, 800/Hotel-NY or 212/766-6600. www.seaportinn.com, 72 rooms. Fitness room. Restaurant: No.
   This is a pretty hotel with a super downtown location. Complimentary continental breakfast is served each morning and coffee, tea and cookies each afternoon. Bonus: All rooms have refrigerators. Some of the rooms have terraces (not a good idea though with young kids) with views of the Brooklyn Bridge. Rooms are also equipped with Nintendo games.

Embassy Suites Hotel–New York City
   102 North End Avenue, 800/EMBASSY or 212/945-0100, www.embassysuites.com. 463 suites. Restaurant: Yes. Fitness Center. Cinema.
   Location, location, location. Located directly across the street from the World Trade Center, this hotel was forced to shut its doors following 9/11, reopening eight months later. The hotel is one of the best values for families in Manhattan. In addition to being an all-suite property so families can spread out, it's located adjacent to the Battery Park Esplanade, and is in walking distance of boarding areas for the Statue of Liberty and Ellis Island ferry. Tip: Request a suite with waterviews of the Hudson River and the New York Harbor. This hotel is also the official hotel of the Tribeca Film Festival and features an ambitious art collection. The in-suite amenities go the extra mile: think Starbucks Coffee. Bonus: Complimentary full cooked-to-order breakfast served each morning in Brokers Loft and a nightly Manager's Reception with complimentary beverages. The hotel complex also features family-friendly restaurants: Chevy's (a fun Mexican concept), Lily's (Chinese), Pac-Rim (Japanese) and Pick-a Bagel Deli.

SOHO/GREENWICH VILLAGE
EXPENSIVE ***
Tribeca Grand Hotel
   2 Avenue of the Americas, 877/519-6600, www.tribecagrand.co www.tribecagrand.co. 203 rooms. Fitness center. Concierge. Restaurant: Yes.
   Popular with trendsetters, the Tribeca Grand has a great location for

families: walk just four blocks west and you'll hit the five-mile Hudson Park, a 550-acre park which runs along the Hudson River from Battery Park in lower Manhattan to 59th Street. The rooms aren't grand but the hotel's Sunday brunch is: Served in the Church Lounge, buffet-style, the spread features everything from shrimp to sushi to Belgian waffles. The best part, though, for families: free kids' flicks shown throughout the day in the Grand Screen. There's also a coffee/tea/cocoa bar on each floor, as well as a video/compact disc library—and pets are welcome.

Soho Grand Hotel
310 West Broadway, 800/965-3000, www.sohogrand.com. 367 rooms. Restaurant: Yes.

A 17-story high hotel that the fashion and entertainment industry love. The hotel is also a favorite watering hole of dogs—thanks to the stone dog fountain outside the hotel's entrance. And, in addition to amenities for guests, petamenities. Oh, did we mention that the Soho Grand is partly owned by Hartz Mountain Industries (as is its sister property, the Tribeca Grand). A gourmet menu is served in what the hotel calls "Soho's Living Room," also known as the Grand Bar and Lounge; it is a place to see and be seen.

MODERATE **
Washington Square Hotel
103 Waverly Place, 800/222-0418, 212/777-9515, www.washingtonsquarehotel.com. 140 rooms. Exercise room. Concierge. Restaurant: Yes.

My mother's friends from Boston always stay at this "find" while visiting New York. The hotel is reminiscent of something you'd find in Europe: not much in the way of frills, yet clean and comfortable. Complimentary breakfast is served each morning in the bistro-like restaurant, which is a much-sought after spot for dinner by locals and tourists. Bonus: Washington Square Park sits directly across the street.

MEATPACKING DISTRICT
VERY EXPENSIVE ****
Hotel Gansevoort
18 Ninth Avenue (at 13th Street; considered the Meatpacking District, 877/726-7386, www.hotelgansevoort.com. 207 rooms and suites. Restaurant: Yes. Concierge. Spa and fitness center.

If your kids must have a pool, this pricey hotel has a 45-foot heated rooftop pool with piped-in underwater music. Bliss. Another nice thing going for this property is a roof garden and its pretty city and river views. The décor is modern with a twist—eel skin columns, mohair panels and leather and velvet accents set the scene. Bonus: The hotel is pet-friendly; and there's even canine-friendly

Doggie DayCare located right across the street, as well as Hudson River Park playground a dog bone's throw away. The guestrooms feel roomy, thanks to nine-foot ceilings; feather beds are in each room. The restaurant is Japanese, which can be somewhat limiting if you don't love Japanese food. However, the hotel is steps away from Pastis and other fun, lively restaurants in the Meatpacking District.

CHELSEA
EXPENSIVE ***
Maritime Hotel
363 West 16th Street, 212/242-4300, www.themaritimehotel.com, 124 rooms and suites. Fitness center. Restaurant: Yes.

Your first clue that this is the Maritime Hotel are the porthole windows. If you'll be traveling as a single parent with one child this property will work; otherwise the standard rooms are too small for a cot and you'll need to swing for a suite. However, the outdoor café is a hot spot for visitors and locals on a nice day.

INEXPENSIVE *
Hampton Inn Manhattan/Chelsea
108 West 24th Street, 800/HAMPTON or 212/414-1000, www.hamptoninn.com. 144 rooms. Fitness room. Restaurant: No.

This 20-story high rise is no-frills, with the exception of the complimentary breakfast bar in the mornings and free coffee and tea in the lobby 24 hours a day.

THEATER DISTRICT/TIMES SQUARE
EXPENSIVE ***
New York Marriott Marquis
1535 Broadway, 212/39801900, www.nymarriottmarquis.com.1,946 rooms. Fitness Center. Restaurant: Yes

The Marriott Marquis is practically a city within a city with seven restaurants and a tour/transportation desk. The hotel is centrally located in the thick of all the Times Square action. Bonus: And it's got New York's only revolving lounge and restaurant. Kids love the fact that if you get up to go to the bathroom your table will be in a different spot when you return. Even if you opt not to stay here, take the kids to visit the revolving lounge for a couple of Shirley Temples and Roy Rogers; brunch and dinner are also served.

Crowne Plaza Times Square Manhattan
1605 Broadway, 800/243-6969 or 212/977-4000, www.manhattan.crowneplaza.com. 770 rooms and suites. Fitness center. Restaurant: Yes.

Ker-ching: A swimming pool is one of the lures for families. In-room video games are another. A busy spot with lots going on in the thick of it all.

The Westin New York at Times Square

270 West 43rd Street (8th Avenue), 212/201-2700 or 866/837-4183, www.westinny.com. 863 rooms Fitness center and spa. Restaurant: Yes. Weekend and seasonal packages.

Steps from The Lion King, Toys 'R Us, the Yankee Clubhouse and one of the largest Mickey D's (McDonald's) anywhere, this hotel is kids' headquarters. The 45-story hotel's façade with streaks of purple and blue is even pleasing to kids. The youngest children are greeted with a gift bag that includes a coloring book, crayons, a Westin cup and Westin hat. Teen girls will *ooh* and *ahh* over the Teen/Tween Spa Menu at the spa, with treatments like the Velvet Glow Facial and the Skin Dew body treatment. Bonus: The chain's Heavenly Beds and Heavenly Bath products are in all guestrooms.

W New York Times Square

1567 Broadway (at 47th Street), 212/930-7400, www.starwood.com. 511 rooms. Concierge. Health club.

If there aren't many of you traveling (translation: one parent, one child), this is a fun hotel for kids and adults. But rooms are teeny weeny. A nice touch: The Whatever/Whenever policy—if you need something (within reason), just push the Whatever/Whenever button on the phone. The décor is very trendy and so is the clientele. Note: There are five W Hotels in the City. I personally love the W Hotels but if you've got a brood or are prone to claustrophobia, stay elsewhere (unless you can swing for a suite or two guestrooms).

MODERATE **
Doubletree Guest Suites Times Square New York City

1568 Broadway, 800/325-9033 or 212/719-1600, www.doubletree.com. 460 suites. Restaurant: Yes. Fitness room. Concierge.

In a word: Suite. In a city where space is a rarity, a hotel that offers all suites for the cost of a standard room elsewhere is appreciated. Separate living rooms (with pullout sofa beds), dining/work areas and bedroom, refrigerator, microwave, coffeemaker, 2 TV's...home away from home. A kid's menu and a vacation station round out the family-friendly theme.

Courtyard by Marriott–Manhattan/Times Square South

114 West 40th Street, 800/228-9290 or 212/391-0088, www.courtyardtimessquare.com. 244 rooms. Fitness center. Exercise room. Pets allowed. Concierge. Restaurant: Yes.

A pet friendly and kid-friendly 32-story property with a complimentary breakfast buffet in the courtyard café. Complimentary coffee served in the lobby 24/7.

Millennium Broadway Hotel New York

145 West 44th Street, 800/622-5569 or 212/768-4400, www.millenniumhotels.com. 750 rooms. Concierge. Restaurant: Yes.

Your dog or cat can stay at this very large hotel with tons of activity in the thick of the action.

Hotel 41

206 West 41st Street, 212/703-8600 or 877-847-4444, www.hotel41.com. 47 rooms. Restaurant: Yes.

Located next door to the Nederlander Theater, home to the long-running musical Rent, Hotel 41 is a boutique property with some nice touches. Complimentary espresso and cappuccino are offered daily between 4 and 7pm, and complimentary breakfast is available daily between 7am and 11am. Bonus: Pet friendly. A CD/DVD lending library is also on premises. Guestroom amenities feature Belgian bed linens and bottled spring water.

Parent Tip

It's no secret, of course, that New York City is pricey. Not only are the hotels and restaurants expensive but the little things like a cup of coffee, a soda or lemonade and snacks that growing kids always seem to shout for all add up and take a big bite out of the family vacation budget. Suggestion: If the hotel you are interested in staying has a club floor, consider going for it. It'll cost more than a guestroom on a "regular" floor, but you get more than what you pay for. For example, the Crowne Plaza Times Square Manhattan hotel's Crowne Plaza Club Floor offers guests complimentary breakfast, afternoon snacks, evening hors 'd oeuvres, non-alcoholic beverages (cappuccino, espresso, sodas and juices available all day), and newspapers. Plus, there's a lounge that you can consider your living room when thing seem tight in the guestroom. Think about it: If you take advantage of the offerings, you can save a pretty bundle. Plus, on most hotel Club Floors, you'll get personalized attention and niceties from the Club Floor concierge. These special floor levels are especially popular with business travelers—and can be a great bonus for families—and many hotels offer them.

MIDTOWN

VERY EXPENSIVE ★★★★

The Four Seasons Hotel New York

57 East 57th Street (at Park and Madison Avenues), 212/758-5700, www.fourseasons.com/newyorkfs, 364 rooms and suites. Restaurant: Yes. Spa.

Designed by I.M. Pei, this stark, yet striking midtown hotel, always a chic place for business travelers, has recently begun to woo family travelers in a big way. The Kids for All Seasons package offers adjoining rooms at a 50 percent discount. The package includes: a "You Can Do Anything in New York" children's brochure that features attractions, activities and restaurants for kids. Kid-friendly amenities are offered to kids ages four to 17 years old. They include: age appropriate toys, bath amenities (sponge letters) and a food and beverage snack or sweet such as personalized Strawberry Pop Tarts and chocolate strawberries and chocolate milk for the little ones and root beer, Toblerone bars and a "Kids Take New York" guidebook for teens. Kids menus are offered in the restaurant and room service.

Bonus: The concierge desk stocks a complimentary video library with children and teen videos and each guestroom has a Sony Play Station.

The Plaza Hotel
768 Fifth Avenue (59th Street), 800/257-7544 or 212/759-3000, www.fairmont.com. 805 rooms and suites. Spa. Restaurant: Yes.

If your little girl mimics Eloise, *"Ooooooo, I absolutely love The Plaza,"* she'll flip over The Eloise Experience package. Included in the package: three nights accommodations; complimentary membership in the Young Plaza ambassadors (valued at $500; for more info about the Young Plaza ambassadors go to www.plazaypa.com); complimentary ice cream sundaes in The Palm Court for up to two children; a choice of complimentary valet parking or a $30 food and beverage credit per night; and a signed photo of Eloise. The rates begin at $289 per night (up to two children per guestroom).

Bonus: The Plaza is located at the heel of Central Park and across the street from FAO Schwarz Toy Store. The moody Oak Room, a New York institution, is a special spot for a drink—my son even felt the significance of the room.

EXPENSIVE ***
Le Parker Meridien New York
118 West 57th Street, 800/543-4300 or 212/245-5000, www.parkermeridien.com. 730 rooms and suites. Restaurant: Yes.

Get this: Before even setting foot in the Big Apple, kids can check-in with a virtual New York smart aleck concierge at http://parkermeridien.com/aleck.htm. After reservations are made, kids visit the website to find out what's happening when they'll be in town and to fill in info about what makes them tick.

Even the elevators at this hotel speak to kids; cartoons and comedy shows entertain them on the ride up and down.

Hate to leave Iggy the Lizard behind? The hotel welcomes pets of all sizes. Really. And they've even got a special pet room service menu with things like birdseed.

Kids Kardio Classes are held at the hotel's gravity fitness and spa; classes include Jazzercise, a movement class. If that doesn't blow off enough steam, the free loaner Razor Scooter might. The penthouse pool overlooking Central Park speaks to kids and adults.

Calling all kids: The hotel's restaurant, Norma's, features breakfast all day. Think: Super Cheesy French Toast and Waz-Za waffles for breakfast. Or, for total anonymity, check out the no name, no sign burger joint where burgers, fries and shakes are chowed and slurped. Visit here on Sunday and kids are in for a real treat at Seppi's Sunday choco-mania chocolate brunch.

Guestrooms are done up in slick cherry and cedar woods and have CD/DVD players.

The Alex Hotel

205 East 45th Street, 212/867-5100, www.thealexhotel.com. 203 rooms. Concierge. Fitness room. Restaurant: Yes.

Named for my son Alex (kidding), this chic hotel makes a statement with limestone baths, Frederic Fekkai bathamenities and a Japanese restaurant. Guest rooms are feng shui inspired in décor and design.

Algonquin Hotel

59 West 44th Street, 888/304-2047 or 212/840-6800, www.algonquinhotel.com. 174 rooms and suites. Concierge. Fitness center. Restaurant: Yes.

An historic hotel, you can practically taste the tradition. The Round Table Room, where literary types would spend legendary liquid lunches discussing who knows what, is still here with its cushy velvet chairs. Antique furniture and writing desks punctuate the lobby and the original marble stairs have been restored. I spent the night here before attending the Harvard Club wedding (down the street) of Ted Demme, popular filmmaker (and nephew of Jonathan Demme) who tragically died not long after. Guestrooms are small but not cookie cutter.

Avalon

16 East 32nd Street, 212/299-7000, 888/HI-AVALON, www.theavalonny.com. 100 rooms and suites. Restaurant: Yes.

Not located in the most popular of neighborhoods, yet not far from Macy's and the Empire State Building, the Avalon is a tony address. A library/club room, imported Italian marble bathrooms and complimentary access to nearby Bally's Sports Club are some of its best features. Complimentary breakfast is included in the rate. The main reason to book this hotel: 80 of the 100 guestrooms are suites.

The Benjamin

125 East 50th Street, 212/715-2500, www.affinia.com. Fitness Center and Spa, Concierge. Restaurant: Yes.

We stayed here the night before my son performed a piano recital at Carnegie Hall and had a great night's sleep (rooms are soundproof) and enjoyable stay. All of the rooms are suites—which, for families is a boon. Some nice touches: A sleep concierge with a pillow menu (you choose the type of pillow you want), and a Hasbro game cart and video library. Bonus: A Grandparent's Package that includes a one-bedroom suite, coupons to kid-friendly attractions and restaurants and Power Paks (pretzels, popcorn, etc.) are included for $205 per night. Note: The Benjamin is part of the Affinia collection of hotels (see sidebar).

MODERATE **

The Fitzpatrick Grand Central Hotel

141 East 44th Street (at Lexington Avenue), 800/367-7701, www.fitzpatrickgrandcentralhotel.com, 155 rooms and suites. Restaurant: Yes.

If your last name begins with an "O," or you're fond of Ireland, this hotel is your lucky four leaf clover. Owned by an Irish company, the Fitzpatrick Grand Central is the sister property to The Fitzpatrick Manhattan (see separate listing). This hotel serves Irish breakfast all day long in its Irish pub, the Wheeltapper, as well as pub grub. Bonus: The hotel is located steps from Grand Central Station. Guestrooms feature pretty canopied beds.

Fitzpatrick Manhattan

Lexington Avenue, 800/367-7701, www.fitzpatrickmanhattanhotel.com. 92 rooms and suites. Health club access. Restaurant: Yes.

The first of the NYC Fitzpatrick hotels (there are two, the other is The Fitzpatrick Grand Central Hotel), this property's got some nice touches, including turndown service with Irish mineral water and chocolates. Bonus: Irish breakfast is served all day long (7am to 10:30 daily) in the hotel's Fitzer's restaurant. And, guests can take advantage of complimentary access to a local health and fitness club. For kids: Pay-per-view movies and Nintendo, as well as VCR's upon request.

Jolly Hotel Madison Towers NY

38th and Madison Avenue, 212/802-0600, www.jollymadison.com. 244 rooms, including junior suites. Spa. Concierge. Restaurant: Yes.

Expect to be greeted with *bongiorno* or *ciao bella* instead of good morning at this Italian-flavored boutique hotel that features all things Italian, including an Italian-speaking staff, newspapers, an Italian breakfast cafe with pretty red tulip chairs and granite tables and an Italian restaurant. For kids, guestrooms feature Nintendo.

Novotel New York
226 West 52nd Street (at Broadway), 212/315-0100, www.novotel.com 480 rooms. Fitness room. Restaurant: Yes.
Novotel has a mascot dolphin named Dolfi. Kids check-in at the Dolfi corner where they'll find a Lego table and a television/VCR and they'll receive a Dolfi figure. The hotel's restaurants give kids a placemat, a beaker with a straw and a game or puzzle; there's also a Children's menu.
One of the cool things about this hotel is that you can sit at one of the tiered terraces at the hotel's 7th floor Broadway Bar and Lounge to enjoy al fresco dining and views of Times Square.
The hotel is centrally located and within walking distance of Lincoln Center, Radio City Music Hall, Carnegie Hall and Central Park.

Crown Plaza at United Nations
304 East 42nd Street, 212/986-8800, www.sixcontinentshotels.com. 300 rooms. Concierge. Fitness center and spa. Restaurant: Yes.
A hotel with a swimming pool is one good reason families stay at this historic landmark hotel. Other reasons are its location: a quiet part of town on the edge of Tudor City. Pets are welcome here, too.

Parent Tip
For families on a shoestring budget, there is a collection of hotels, all in midtown, under then brand name of Apple Core. They include: **La Quinta Inn Manhattan,** 17 West 32nd Street; **Red Roof Inn,** 6 West 32nd Street; **Comfort Inn Midtown,** 129 West 46th Street; **Super 8 Hotel Times Square,** 59 West 46th Street; and the **Ramada Inn East Side,** 161 Lexington Avenue. Rates start at these properties at $89 per night, including continental breakfast and kids under the age of 13 stay free. Make no mistake about it, these are budget properties but they do offer in-room video games, coffee makers and space—all five hotels accommodate up to four people in a room and the Super 8 Hotel Times Square features family suites. Bonus: the properties are located within walking distance of the Empire State Building, Times Square and other midtown points of interest.
For more information or reservations for any of the Apple Core properties, call 800/567-7720, 212/790-2719 or visit www.applecorehotels.com.

Radisson Lexington NY

511 Lexington Avenue at 48th Street, 800/333-3333, www.radisson.com, 700 rooms and suites. Fitness center. Concierge. Restaurant: Yes.

This modern property housed in a 1920's shell speaks to families with a collection of suites—with tons of room—and large-enough-for-a-family-of-four deluxe guestrooms. Heads up grandparents: The hotel chain offers "Senior Breaks" which allows guests 50 years old and older a discounted rate of 25 percent off rack rates.

Affinia Hotels

There is a cool collection of hotels in the City under the umbrella company, Affinia. These properties are all suite hotels and a great value for families—they range from very pricey to moderately priced. They include:

- **Affinia Dumont**
150 East 34th Street, 212/481-7600
- **The Benjamin**
(see separate write-up)
- **Beekman Tower Hotel**
3 Mitchell Place (at 49th and 1st), 212/355-7300
- **Eastgate Tower**
222 East 39th Street, 212/687-8000
- **Lyden Gardens**
215 East 64th Street, 212/355-1230
- **Plaza Fifty**
155 East 50th Street, 212/751-5710
- **Shelburne Murray Hill**
303 Lexington Avenue, 212/689-5200
- **Southgate Tower**
371 Seventh Avenue, 212/563-1800
- **Surrey Hotel**
(see separate listing)

UPPER EAST SIDE
VERY EXPENSIVE ****
The Pierre New York

Fifth Avenue (at 61t street), 800/332-3442, www.fourseasons.com/pierre. Fitness center. Concierge. Fitness center. Restaurant: Yes.

A Four Seasons property that overlooks Central Park, The Pierre wows kids with several packages. Le Petit Pierre Weekend Package includes special vouchers that allows kids VIP entrance into the Museum of Natural History and tickets to the Space Show at the Rose Center for Earth and Space. Additionally, kids can create their own fantasy concoction of a pound of candy at Dylan's Candy Bar, the hottest candy store in town and just a gumball's throw from the hotel.

The package also features: one night in a Deluxe King guest room or a Deluxe Suite (both provide an extra connecting twin room), breakfast for two adults and children's breakfast menu, one pay-per-view movie, popcorn and soda, cookies and milk at turndown each evening and a goodie bag with complimentary tickets to the Central Park Zoo (located across the street), a Beanie toy, choice of New York coloring book or, for older kids, postcards and pens, a children's walking map of the City and a copy of *Museums for Families* magazine. Wait, there's more: Families can also request Sony Playstation 2 and games, kid's umbrellas, board games and children's robes or infant's care basket. The package rates begin at $625 per night; the package is available only on weekends and holidays.

The Carlyle

Madison Avenue (at 76th Street), 800/227-5737, 212/744-1600, www.thecarlyle.com. 179 rooms and suites. Restaurant: Yes. Fitness center, concierge.

A grande dame-type hotel, this is one of New York's most elegant hideaways with rich carpets, chintz drapery and traditional décor. Try and get a room that overlooks Central Park. The fact that the hotel is steps from the Park is also a draw for families who can consider it their backyard for the duration of their stay.

The Stanhope, A Park Hyatt Hotel

995 5th Avenue (at 81st Street), 212/774-1234, www.hyatt.com. 130 rooms and suites. Concierge. Health club. Restaurant: Yes.

I love the sidewalk café at the Stanhope, which sits directly across the street from the Metropolitan Museum of Art (open April through October). The tony address alone speaks volumes about the elegant and desirable Stanhope. Another plus: Pets are welcome here. The guestrooms are large (relatively speaking in a town where space is a privilege, not a right). Still, the suites guarantee even more breathing room and are not that much pricier. There's an afternoon tea in the Library in the winter months.

The Regency

540 Park Avenue at 61st Street, 212/759-4100, www.loewshotels.com 351 rooms and 85 suites. Fitness center. Restaurant: Yes.

A Park Avenue address hotel that loves kids. It's true! So much so that they get their very own concierge, Kaptain Kid. His real name is Mohammed Pinto and he's been a big brother to kids who stay at the hotel since 1990, from kicking soccer ballls in the hallways to baking cookies in the kitchen to whispering bedtime stories at night. Kaptain Kid will even escort families to FAO Schwartz (located just blocks from the hotel).

When kids check into the hotel they receive a bucket with goodies such as confetti bubble bath, a travel journal and stickers along with a welcome note from Kaptain Kid. The kids also have access to the "Kid's Kloset" which stocks games and books.

This hotel also talks to the fussiest of travelers—teenagers. Teens receive a complimentary "T. Loews"amenity kit that includes a Loews logo bag and drink bottle; suggestions for cool shopping, attractions and activities near the hotel; coupons for a sundae; and samples of trendy teen things like beauty products, magazines and candy. There's also a Did You Forget Closet that stocks Gameboys, DVD Players, CD Players, walkie talkies, teen books, board games and exercise equipment. The icing on the cake: If your teen shudders at the thought of sharing a hotel room and bathroom with his or her family, consider the Teen Suite Package which includes an option to reserve a second room at a rate of $100; it also includes an in-room movie and free popcorn.

MODERATE **
Hotel Wales
1295 Madison Avenue, 212/876-6000, 866-WALES-HOTEL, www.waleshotel.com. Fitness studio.

This century-old hotel is located a stroll's distance away from Central Park and the Metropolitan Museum of Art and the Guggenheim Museum. Nice touches: a signature drink upon arrival, complimentary espresso/cappuccino 24-hours day, complimentary bottle of water, complimentary video/CD library (each room has a VCR), fitness studio and access to the 92nd Street Y ($15 a day). Bonus: Sarabeth's one of the most popular brunch spots for Upper East Siders is located in this hotel. Now, the bad news: the rooms are tiny, so you'll have to book a suite.

The Melrose Hotel New York
One Barbizon Place, Lexington Avenue at 63rd Street, 800/MELROSE, 212/838-5700, www.melrosehotelnewyork.com. 306 rooms and suites. Fitness center and spa. Concierge. Restaurant: Yes.

Once upon a time, this property was the Barbizon, a women's-only residence; Grace Kelly and Candice Bergen once lived here, and so did my college friend Jamie Karp. This property was renovated to the tune of $40 million and is subsequently a luxury property. When I visited Jamie here, the rooms were once so small you couldn't change your mind in them. That's changed; walls were knocked down and today they're big enough to accommodate families. The Equinox Fitness Club and Spa takes over four floors of the hotel. Caveat: Noone under 18 years old is allowed to use its pool.

Surrey Hotel
20 East 76th Street, 212/288-3700, www.affinia.com. 131 rooms and suites. Concierge. Fitness center. Restaurant: Yes.

Every single room or suite at this nothing-fancy-hotel-with-a-fancy-Upper-East-Side-address has a kitchenette or kitchen with a fridge—which can translate to huge savings for a family. One of Manhattan's best restaurants is located downstairs in the Surrey: Café Boulud (pricey but extraordinary). Bonus: As a member of the Affinia hotels, this property offers a Grandparents package.

UPPER WEST SIDE
VERY EXPENSIVE ★★★★
Mandarin Oriental New York
80 Columbus Circle, 212/805-8800, www.mandarinoriental.com. 251 rooms and suites. Spa. Restaurant: Yes.

For some vacationing families, a hotel without a pool is like a vacation without a vacation. This elegant property has a 75-foot naturally lighted indoor lap pool—but it'll cost you as this is one of the most expensive hotels in the city, as well as one of the newest. It makes it home at the top of the swanky Time Warner Center, affording guests with stunning views of Central Park, the City or the Hudson River.

EXPENSIVE ★★★
The Mayflower Hotel on the Park
15 Central Park West (at 61st and 62nd streets), 212/265-0060, http://mayflowerhotel.com. 365 rooms and suites. Fitness center. Concierge. Restaurant: Yes.

Request a guestroom with a view of Central Park and you'll feel rich in this affordable, no-frills property. The rooms are a good size and clean, but it's the Central Park location that has put this hotel on the map as a place to stay in Manhattan. Bonus: Some of the suites have pantries with a refrigerator and sink, and others even have kitchenettes. Complimentary coffee is served in the lobby each morning and refreshments each afternoon.

And Keep an Eye Out For...

As this book went to press, there were a number of new properties on the City horizon, scheduled to open in the near future. They include:

The Blakely New York

136 West 55th Street, 212/245-1800.
A renovated 115-room property, formerly the Gorham Hotel.

70 Park Avenue

70 Park Avenue, 800/70-PARKE, www.70parkavenuehotel.com.
Formerly the Doral Park Avenue Hotel, the Kimpton Hotel Group purchased the 205-room property.

The Metropolitan Hotel

569 Lexington Avenue, 212/752-7000.
This property will be repositioned as a DoubleTree Hotel following a $30 million renovation.

Hampton Inn Manhattan/Midtown-Herald Square

31st Street at Sixth Avenue, 800/HAMPTON.
A 136 property near Macy's and Penn Station.

Hampton Inn Manhattan/Seaport—Financial District

320 Pearl Street, 800/HAMPTON.
A 65-room hotel near South Street Seaport.

Courtyard by Marriott Harlem

125th Street at Park Avenue.
A 204-room hotel.

Chapter 10

FIELD TRIPS

LONG ISLAND

In a word: Beach. Because Long Island is surrounded by water—the Long Island Sound on the North Shore and the Atlantic Ocean on the South—there are more-than-you-can-count sandy strands here for city slickers to worship the sun.

Celebrities and jaded New Yorkers who escape the steamy city heat and the frenetic city beat, travel east from New York City to **The Hamptons**, a sandy playground for the stars. The Hamptons (also known as the Island's South Fork) are also perfect antidotes to the hectic touring pace of the City for tourists—if you have the luxury of time to enjoy both city and sea.

Long Island's **North Fork** has also become a popular getaway in recent years, thanks to its many wineries and sweet villages with hotels, restaurants and farmstands. While the Hamptons are the place to see and be seen for Type A personalities, the scene on the North Fork is for low-profile, low-maintenance sorts.

There's also more to Long Island than the Hamptons and the North Fork. The **Fire Island National Seashore**, a 32-mile barrier island with unspoiled beaches and the Sunken Forest, a 300-year-old holly forest, as well as an historic lighthouse you can tour. The westernmost six miles of Fire Island make up **Robert Moses State Park**, which harbors excellent beaches.

Tourist Information

Long Island Convention & Visitors Bureau and Sports Commission, 330 Motor Parkway, Suite 203, Hauppauge, Long Island, NY 11788, 877/ FUNONLI or visit www.licvb.com.

GETTING THERE

Make no mistake about it Long Island is very much an island. Whether by car or train you'll need to get across the East River, (which separates the City from the Island) via one of seven bridges and tunnels. Note: If you plan to visit the Hamptons, you won't need but you might want a car once you're there because it is spread out.

By Car

Which route to take all depends on where on the Island you choose to go. If you will be traveling all the way to the Hamptons or Montauk (the very end of Long Island), your best bet is to take the Long Island Expressway (I-495) to exit 70 (Manorville). Make a right off the ramp, go to the end and make a left onto Route 27(Sunrise Highway), which will take you to the Hamptons. To get to the North Fork, take the Long Island Expressway (I-495) to Exit 73. At the

Parent Tips

I have three **Hamptons** tips for you:

• Get your hands on the current issue of the slick and informative *Hamptons Family Life* (HFL) magazine, which is distributed free in New York City at restaurants, nail salons, child development centers and other spots. The magazine offers a wealth of info for families who live in or are visiting the Hamptons. Of course, you can also pick up a copy when in The Hamptons.

• If you take the train or Jitney and plan to spend at least one night, the **Southampton Inn** is a great spot. The inn is centrally located in the pretty town of Southampton so you can walk to great shops and restaurants. Bonus: The inn will pick you up at the train or Jitney bus stop, and will also shuttle you to the beach. Family package prices are reasonable. For information or reservations call 800/832-6500 or visit www.southamptoninn.com.

• If you're the parent of little kids (five years old and younger), the cool **Hamptons Baby Beach Club** is a great getaway. The Club is located in the **Atlantic Motel** in Southampton and features a 3-to-5 day midweek program for moms, dads and little tykes. On the agenda: mom and baby yoga, sand castle building, cooking lessons, cocktails and cookies parties...the fun never stops. You check in on a Sunday and check out Thursday. The package includes accommodations, breakfast, lunch, dinner and all activities. The cost: $250 per day for one parent and one child; each additional parent is $50 and each additional child is $25 per day. Note: The program is offered in the summer only. Call 631/283-6100 or visit www.hrhresorts.com.

꙳

bottom of the ramp you're on Route 58 to the east to Orient. The other two main express routes that cross the Island are Northern State Parkway, which runs from Queens to Hauppaugue and Southern State Parkway, which runs from Brooklyn and Queens (this road is also known as the Belt Parkway) to Oakdale.

By Train

The Long Island Rail Road is the nation's largest commuter railroad. It operates 740 passenger trains daily on three major east-west routes from New York City along the entire Nassau-Suffolk County region, with 124 train stations. The LIRR offers summer package tours; call 516/822-LIRR.

WHERE ARE WE GOING NOW?
Jones Beach State Park

Ocean Parkway, Wantagh, 516/785-1600.

I grew up at the incredible beaches here and, as a travel writer now for a very long time have had the privilege of traveling to some of the most incredible beaches: Jones Beach is right up there with the best of them.

The 2,400-acre park features six miles of ocean beach, a bayfront beach (perfect for waders), a two-mile stretch of boardwalk, an outdoor pool and a golf course. Bonus: The Tommy Hilfiger Theater, an outdoor theater where fabulous concerts are put on.

Splish Splash

2549 Splish Splash Drive, P.O. Box 1090, Riverhead, 631/727-3600, www.splishsplashlongisland.com, (Exit 72 West off the Long Island Expressway).

Open: Weekends from Memorial Day weekend to mid-June, then daily from mid-June to Labor Day.

Admission: Adults $27.99 (over 48 inches tall), $20.99 (under 48 inches tall and seniors 65 years and older), kids three years old and younger are free. After 4pm, admission is $20.99 (over 48 inches tall), $16.99 (under 48 inches tall and seniors 65 years and older), kids three years old and younger are free.

The largest water park in New York State, this 96-acre wonderland of water rides makes quite a splash with kids. There's a 1,300-foot-long "lazy river" ride; more than 20 water slides, including the Hollywood Stunt Rider, a totally-in-the-dark family raft ride with steep drops and surprises; a 30,000-gallon Wave Pool; Soak City; Kiddie Cove; Monsoon Lagoon; and daily performances (high dive shows, seal shows and the Great American Bird Show).

Long Island Children's Museum

11 Davis Avenue, Garden City (off Charles Lindbergh Blvd. At Mitchel Center, Exit M4 off the Meadowbrook Parkway), 516/224-5800, www.licm.org. Open: Wednesday through Sunday 10am to 5pm; July and August Tuesday through Sunday 10am to 5pm. Closed major holidays.

Admission: General admission $8, seniors (65 years and older) $7.

Geared for young kids (under 12 years old), this hands-on museum is fun for kids on the Island. But honestly, the children's museums in Manhattan and Brooklyn are great and there's no compelling reason to travel here to visit (unless you'll be in the area). Exhibits include things like the bubble room (my son has spent lots of time here through the years beginning when the museum was housed in a smaller space down the road); a mock TV station and radio station, a hands-on Music Gallery, and a climbing structure, among others.

Cradle of Aviation Museum

1 Davis Avenue, Garden City, 516/572-4111, www.cradleofaviation.org Open: Tuesday 10am to 2pm, Wednesday through Sunday 10am to 5pm Monday and Tuesday during school breaks and holidays open 9:30am to 5pm. Closed Mondays.

Admission: $7 adults, $6 kids, IMAX movies separate admission.

Located right next door to the Long Island Children's Museum this museum is on par with the fabulous Smithsonian Air and Space Museum in Washington, DC—but not as large. The museum sits on the same site where Charles Lindbergh took his historic flight. In addition to really cool exhibits (especially for boys), like an F-11 Tiger and an original 1972 lunar landing module, there is an IMAX Theater with a number of aviation-and-space-related shows.

CONNECTICUT

A compact state, Connecticut is considered to be a part of New England—but the southern part of Connecticut is a much closer sibling to New York than New England. This is because so many of the folks who live in the southern parts of the Nutmeg State work in the Big Apple. Move farther up the coast though, and there's a new chapter to the story with more evidence of New England's Puritan past. It's evident in the cuisine (lobster and chowder), in the accommodations (bed-and-breakfasts and quintessential New England inns) and in the lay of the land (sprawling town greens and a sprinkling of fishing villages).

The state's most popular tourist attraction is **Mystic Seaport**, a step-back-in-time, 19th-century village (about two-and-a-half-hour-drive from Manhattan) where kids can board a historic ship, dress up in period clothing and hoist a sail.

We've named a couple of other family-friendly attractions in the state that are a bit closer to Manhattan for you to consider visiting, but really Mystic Seaport is where it's at for families.

GETTING THERE
By Car
Traveling from the City by car, the most direct route is I-95. However, you'll share the road with tons of tractor-trailers and trucks. An easier route is the Hutchinson and Merritt Parkways, where rule-the-road trucks are banned. Caveat: You'll trade in trucks for deer, as this stretch of road is populated by lots of deer that are known to leap across the road—or at least attempt to.

By Train
Metro North (the New Haven Line) runs between New York City's Grand Central Terminal and New Haven; call 800/638-7646. Note: Metro North offers special excursion packages with round-trip rail service from New York City. The packages are sold by Metro North ticket agents on the day of travel at Grand Central Terminal; call 800/638-7646.

Tourist Information
Southern Connecticut Tourism District, P.O. Box 89, 470 Bank Street, New London, CT 06320, 860/444-2206, www.mysticmore.com. For Connecticut State information, call 800/CT-BOUND.

WHERE ARE WE GOING NOW?
Mystic Seaport
75 Greenmanville Avenue, Rte. 27, Mystic (exit 90 off the I-95), 860-572-5315, 888/SEAPORT.

Mystic Seaport was once a time a proud whaling and shipbuilding center. Today, the seaport is a 17-acre, recreated 19th century seaport village whose attractions include: horse and carriage rides, boat rides and rentals, participatory plays, story-telling, sail-handling demonstrations, hands-on activities for children and the Seaport Gallery.

We've been to Mystic many times and each time we discover something new. Our most recent trip there, on a hot July afternoon, we stumbled across a casual and funny audience-interactive performance on one of the lawn areas at the Seaport. We sat on a bench to cool off and stayed for the show.

Grab a bite to eat in the little town of Mystic at Mystic Pizza on West Main Street (860/536-3700). This pizza joint is where Julia Roberts played her breakout role in the movie by the same name. Although it served pizza before the movie was even conceived, Ms. Roberts put this eatery on the map and it could be argued vice versa. The menu: pizza, spaghetti, hamburgers and grinders.

If you've rented a car and plan to stay more than one day (not a bad idea since it's a two-and-a-half-hour's drive, without traffic), plant yourselves at the **Inn at Mystic**, which overlooks busy Mystic Harbor and Long Island Sound; call 800/237-2415. Or, travel about a half hour inland and spend the night at the **Mohegan Sun** (877/204-7100, www.mohegansun.com). Of course, the kids can't gamble at this casino resort, but they'll have fun in the pool and there's a terrific kids' center they'll enjoy while you grab a bite to eat—you'll have a huge selection from which to choose.

Note: the interior of the hotel is reminiscent of a mall with tons of shops, restaurants and a couple of bars. Smoking is permitted in this "mall," and on a busy weekend, the smoke tends to linger.

The Barnum Museum

820 Main Street, Bridgeport, CT, 203/331-1104, www.barnum-museum.org.

Admission: $5 adults, $4 seniors and students, $3 kids (ages 4 to 18), kids under 4 years old are free.

Open: Tuesday through Saturday 10am to 4:30pm, Sunday noon to 4:30pm, closed Mondays.

Your kids want to join the circus? Or, are they on their way to being nominated class clown? This historical museum might pique their interest with its permanent miniature circus model and story of P.T. Barnum's life and the influence he had on 19th century America.

Stamford Museum and Nature Center

39 Scofieldtown Road, Stamford, 203/322-1646, www.stamfordmuseum.org.

Admission: Adults $6, kids and seniors under the age of 14 $2, kids three years old and under are free.

Open: Monday through Saturday 9am to 5pm, Sunday 11am to 5pm. Nature's playground is open weather permitting. Heckscher Farm is open 9am to 4pm.

A 10-acre working New England farm, visitors can participate in farm chores (woo hoo!), as well as spy interesting animals like Black Welsh mountain lambs. There are also herb and vegetable gardens and woodland trails that kids can explore.

A museum houses five galleries with exhibits depicting Native American culture, fine art and natural history. Bonus: The stars come out on Sunday in the Planetarium. On Friday nights you can check out the solar system with a research telescope at the observatory.

WESTCHESTER

Westchester County sits just to the City's north and is home to some of the most upscale villages and towns in the metro area. Many commuters to the City live in this neck of the woods, drawn to Westchester's tranquility and beauty.

GETTING THERE
By Car
Westchester is about 25 miles from Manhattan, but during rush hour it will seem like a distance of 250 miles. (See individual listings for getting there by car information.)

By Train
Join the throngs of commuters who use the railways to get in and out of Manhattan each day and weekend. Metro-North has 43 station stops in Westchester on three separate lines. The railroad operates continuous services to Grand Central Station in Manhattan. For prices and schedules call 800/ METRO-INFO or visit www.mta.nyc.ny.us/mnr.

Tourist Information
The Westchester County Office of Tourism, 222 Mamaroneck Avenue, Suite 100, White Plains, 800/833-9282 or 914/995-8500, www.westchestertourism.com.
Westchester Arts Council, 914/328-ARTS, www.westarts.com. The Arts Council has information about children's concerts, theater and entertainment throughout Westchester.
Westchester County Department of Parks, Recreation and Conservation, 914/864-PARK, www.westchestergov.com/parks.

WHERE ARE WE GOING NOW?
Playland Amusement Park
Rye, New York, 914/813-7000, www.ryeplayland.org. Traveling by car from the City, take the New England Thruway (I-95) to Exit 19 in Rye. There is a parking fee. Or, take Metro-North's Excursion Package to Playland; 800/METROINFO, www.mta.nyc.ny.us.
Open: May (Weekends to Memorial Day), Saturday noon to 11pm; Sunday noon to 8pm; Spring Season (Memorial Day to late June) Wednesday and Thursday 10am to 4pm, Friday 10am to midnight, Saturday noon to midnight and Sunday noon to 11pm. (Closed Mondays and Tuesdays, except Memorial Day); Summer Season (Late June through Labor Day) Tuesday to Thursday noon to 11pm, Friday and Saturday noon to midnight, Sunday noon to 11pm; Post Labor Day (Select weekends in September), Saturday noon to 9pm, Sunday noon to 8pm.
Admission: Free. However, the rides require tickets. You can purchase booklets of tickets: a 24-ticket book is $21, a 16-ticket book is $17, an 8-ticket book is $9 and a single ticket is $1.25. Note: Most rides are two-to-four tickets each; Kiddieland rides are two tickets each.

Playland isn't as big as Six Flags in New Jersey, and that's part of its appeal. This Art Deco amusement park dates to 1928 and claims to be the country's first plannedamusement park. It butts the Long Island Sound and includes much more than just rides and amusements. There's a beach and pool, miniature golf and many special events throughout the year including fireworks, big band concerts and puppet shows. The rides are what the kids really love and seven of the most popular rides date back to the park's original 1928 date: The Dragon Coaster, Carousel, Derby Races, Old Mill, Whip, Kiddy Coaster and Kiddy Carousel. New rides include the Crazy Mouse Coaster, Playland Plunge, Power Surge and Dream Machine.

Historic Hudson Valley

150 White Plains Road, Tarrytown, NY 10591, 914/631/8200, www.hudsonvalley.org. You can explore Sleepy Hollow Country by traveling Route 9 by car. The region is about 25 miles from Manhattan. Better yet, explore the region on the Sleepy Hollow Cruise run by NY Waterway. Call 800/53-FERRY, www.nywaterway.com. Or, take the Sleepy Hollow Excursion on a Metro-North train. Call 800/METRO-INFO. The Kykuit Visitor Center at Philipsburg Manor in Sleepy Hollow is 914/631/3992.

This region is steeped in history and there is a collection of interesting historic sites that are worthwhile exploring if your family is especially keen on learning about America's history. The picturesque Hudson Valley, especially the 10 miles stretch along the east bank of the Hudson River known as Sleepy Hollow Country, is a nice antidote to the city's concrete and steel landscape. The historic sites here include the following:

Kykuit, the Rockefeller Estate

Sleepy Hollow, 914/631/9491, www.hudsonvalley.org. See Historic Hudson Valley directions above for getting to the area.

Open: daily from May through October, except Tuesdays.

Once upon a time, this estate inspired Washington Irving's tale, *The Legend of Sleepy Hollow* (he also wrote *Rip Van Winkle*). Today, the six-story stone estate is a part of the National Trust for Historic Preservation. The property was originally built by John D. Rockefeller, the American philanthropist, and his son John D. Rockefeller, Jr. Yet, there is much more to Kykuit than the estate. The views of the Hudson are commanding and the gardens are works of art. One of the most celebrated gardens here is Governor Nelson A. Rockefeller's 20th century sculpture collection—think Alexander Calder, Pablo Picasso and Henry Moore. You can tour the property on your own, which we recommend because, while the guided tours are fascinating, they will not captive your children's attention.

Note: Visits to Kykuit begin at the Philipsburg Manor (see listing below) where visitors see an introductory video and then travel to Kykuit by shuttle van. You must provide a car seat for children four years old and younger for the shuttle ride. Also, note, that the tours are not appropriate for children under the age of 10 years old.

Philipsburg Manor

Route 9, Sleepy Hollow, 914/631/3992, www.hudsonvalley.org. See Historic Hudson Valley directions above for getting to the area.

Open: in the summer, 10am to 5pm, daily except Tuesday. Winter hours (November and December) are 10am to 4pm, daily except Tuesday. Closed January and February.

An 18th century farm and gristmill that was restored by John D. Rockefeller, Jr. Kids get a kick out of the oxen, cows and sheep. There is a café here that is open seasonally.

Sunnyside

West Sunnyside Lane, Tarrytown, 914/591-8763, www.hudsonvalley.org Located just a few miles down the road from Philipsburg Manor. See Historic Hudson Valley directions above for getting to the area.

Open: Summer hours are 10am to 5pm, closed Tuesday. Winter hours (November and December), 10am to 4pm, closed Tuesday. Closed January and February. March hours, Saturday to Sunday 10am to 4pm.

Sunnyside is Washington Irving's waterfront home. Bonus: Educational children's tours are given at selected times throughout the year.

The Union Church of Pocantico Hills

Route 448, Bedford Rd., Sleepy Hollow, 914/631/8200, www.hudsonvalley.org. See Historic Hudson Valley directions above for getting to the area.

Open: Take a tour of the church windows April through December, everyday except Tuesday: Monday, Wednesday, Thursday and Friday 11am to 5pm, Saturday 10am to 5pm and Sunday 2pm to 5pm (unless there are church activities). Closed January through March.

This small church is one of the prettiest in the country. The building itself is small and charming. Yet, what really knocks me out are the stained glass windows by Marc Chagall and Henri Matisse, commissioned by members of the Rockefeller family.

Van Cortlandt Manor .

South Riverside Avenue, Croton-on-Hudson, 914/271-8981, www.hudsonvalley.org. See Historic Hudson Valley directions above for getting to the area.

Open: Summer hours, 10am to 5pm, closed Tuesday; Winter hours (November and December), weekends 10am to 4pm. Closed January through March.

Reminiscent of something you'd find in Colonial Williamsburg, this 18th century complex includes a tavern, a tenant farmer's house and a manor house. You can take a tour led by costumed guides to see open-hearth cooking demonstrations and other examples of post Revolutionary War ways of life. There is also a picnic area.

NEW JERSEY

Not unlike Long Island, Connecticut and Westchester, New Jersey is also home to many bedroom communities with commuters to NYC. If you are fortunate enough to have a long vacation to New York City, you might consider visiting the Garden State. But it's not "gardens" kids will want to see here. Instead, kids and families will be interested in checking out three attractions: The Liberty Science Center, Six Flags Great Adventure and Sandy Hook Gateway National Recreation Area.

Tourist Information
New Jersey Travel & Tourism, 800-VISITNJ, www.state.nj.us/travel.

WHERE ARE WE GOING NOW?
Liberty Science Center
251 Phillip Street, Liberty State Park, Jersey City, 201/200-1000. By train from Manhattan, take the PATH train from Penn Station to the Pavonia-Newport or Exchange Place station in Jersey City. Transfer to the Hudson-Bergen Light Rail traveling toward East 34th Street or West Side Avenue. Exit at Liberty State Park station and walk less than a block to Liberty Science Center. Time: About an hour. By car from Manhattan: Take the New Jersey Turnpike to Exit 14B. By ferry: The NY Waterway Ferry leaves from lower Manhattan; call 800/53-FERRY.

Open: Call or visit the website for updated hours.

Admission: Individual passes include Discovery Pass to exhibit floors only (adults $10, seniors and kids ages two to 18 years old $8); IMAX Dome only (adults $9, seniors and kids ages two to 18 years old $7); 3-D Theater only (adults $3.50, seniors and kids ages two to 18 years old $3). Combination passes include: An Expedition Pass which includes the Exhibit Floors, the IMAX Dome and the 3-D Theater (adults $16.50, seniors and kids two to 18 years old $14.50); Adventurer Pass which includes the Exhibit Floors and IMAX Dome (adults $14.50, seniors and kids ages two to 18 years old $12.50); and a Voyager Pass which includes the Exhibit Floors and the 3-D Theater (adults $12, seniors and kids ages two to 18 years old $10).

The Liberty Science Center is a touchy-feely museum for kids. The exhibits here have a welcome twist. At the Environment Floor, kids learn about the earth—by climbing a 20-foot Rock Wall that's studded with fossils and other neat discovery stuff and by peering into a Solar Telescope to learn about the

Bernoulli effect. The Environment Floor also includes a Touch Tank as part of an exhibit called The Estuary. There's an Invention Floor that'll have your kids begging you to patent their next invention. The Health Floor teaches kids about their bodies, while encouraging them to live healthy lifestyles. This science museum is determined to be hands-on and offers a Discovery Room at each of the exhibits where activities are guided by in-the-know staff and volunteers. There's also a LOL Science Demonstration Stage where shows are presented throughout the day. If your kids are homesick, bring them to the Geographical Information System where they can zoom in to see their neighborhood as photographed from space. What really wins over the I-wish-I-was-back-home teen market is the Virtual Sports exhibit. Guests take on virtual opponents in basketball, volleyball, snowboarding or undersea diving, thanks to a video gesture recognition system.

Pre-teens and teens also love the IMAX Dome Theater's 80-foot high screen. The films rotate on a regular basis. Another really cool program, especially appreciated by hard-to-please teens, is the Joseph D. Williams Science Theater, which features colorful lasers in 3-D.

Pre-med or pre-pre-med students will find the Health Floor's Live from ...Cardiac Classroom interesting (or it may sway them to join the circus instead). The exhibit takes place in a small theater and features periodic, real time presentations of cardiac surgery through a multimedia presentation. Really cool: Thanks to teleconferencing technology, kids can pose questions to the operating staff while following the progress of surgery. And get this, kids can even play doctor by suturing an incision and using state-of-the-art MRI and CT scans on a computer at the Medical Imaging Station. The best part: In the Health Floor's Discovery Room, kids can try on an "Empathy Belly" to experience first-hand how it feels to be nine months pregnant.

In the warm months, plan to eat outside at one of the outdoor picnic areas and decks—the views across the river of lower Manhattan are an exhibit in their own right.

Let's face it, this science museum has stiff competition from the American Museum of Natural History and Rose Center across the river in Manhattan, with its worldwide rep as being the best. But what's unique about its New Jersey counterpart is that it's hands-on, and encourages kids to climb, feel and smell their way through the exhibits. If you've got a week of rainy days or cold weather that dictate for indoor activities this museum is worth the one-hour trip across the river from Manhattan.

If your time is limited, or your itinerary shares indoor time with outdoor time thank to great weather, the Liberty Science Museum is a trip you probably can skip, instead opting to spend more time in Manhattan's museums and attractions. It's a shame, though, because this science museum is in a class of its own.

Six Flags Great Adventure

Route 537, Jackson, New Jersey, 732/928-2000, www.sixflags.com. By car, take the George Washington Bridge, Lincoln Tunnel or Holland Tunnel to New Jersey Turnpike South to exit 7A. Proceed to I-195 east to exit 16A, then one mile west on Rte. 537 to Six Flags.

By bus: There are New Jersey Transit buses to the theme park; call 800/ 626-7433.

Open: Call or visit the website for updated hours.

Admission: Prices are subject to change each season. In 2004, the prices for the Theme Park were: Regular $45.99, Junior (under 54 inches) $29.99, Seniors $29.99. Admission to all Six Flags parks: Regular $60.99, Junior (54 inches and under) $45.99 and Senior (55 years and older) $45.99. (If you buy tickets online and save money.

This theme park has been around the block—I came here on prom weekend (at that time, it was called just Great Adventure). Today, many years later, it's still the cool place to go for teens, as well as the littlest ones, thanks to new attractions tailor-sized like Looney Tunes Seaport (six-acres of Bugs Bunny and friends rides and Koala Canyon, a 1/2 acre water play area).

For older kids and teens, the 13 roller coasters are wild and will whet their appetites for rebellious fun. There are also daily shows and parades and nightly fireworks.

Bonus: Right next door to this theme park is Six Flags Hurricane Harbour and Six Flags Wild Safari. Hurricane Harbour is a 45-acre complex with a million-gallon wave pool, river rides and 20 speed slides.

Six Flags Wild Safari insists it's the world's largest drive-thru safari outside of Africa. Over 1,200 animals representing 52 species from around the globe call this safari home (giraffes, monkeys, elephants, rhinos, oh my!). Keep in mind: You'll need to have a car to cruise through the safari.

Sandy Hook Gateway National Recreation Area

National Park Service, Gateway National Recreation Area, Sandy Hook Unit, P.O Box 530, Fort Hancock, New Jersey, 07732, 732/872-0115, www.nps.gov/gate/. Getting here really is half the fun if you choose to do so by NY Waterway. Catch the boat at West 38th Street or the World Financial Center and kick back for the 60-minute ride to Fort Hancock's army base at Sandy Hook. Next up, you'll jump on a bus, which will take you to the beach (it makes stops at all six beaches, you get off where you want). The NY Waterway ferries leave only on Saturday and Sunday mornings. Cost: Roundtrip tickets, adults $27, $13 kids. For more information call 800/53-FERRY or visit www.nywaterway.com. For information about other public transportation to Sandy Hook, call 718/354-4606 or visit www.nps.gov.

Open: The Visitor's Center is open year-round 10am to 5pm. The beach is open sunrise to sunset.

Admission: Gateway has no entrance fees. However, beach parking fees are charged at Sandy Hook (732-872-5970) during the summer.

One of the prettiest stretches of beach along the Jersey Shore, Sandy Hook also is home to the oldest lighthouse still in use (1764) and Fort Hancock. There is also a small museum here, but let's face it, New Yorkers don't escape the summer heat and make the hour-and-a-half-drive to go to a museum (not when they live in a town that's museum central). New Yorkers head here for a taste of sun and surf. There is a necklace of strands; some have bathrooms and food concessions. There are also hiking trails.

INDEX

Things Change!

Phone numbers, prices, addresses, quality of food, etc, all change. If you come across any new information, we'd appreciate hearing from you. No item is too small! Drop us an email note at: Jopenroad@aol.com, or write us at:

New York City with Kids
Open Road Publishing, P.O. Box 284
Cold Spring Harbor, NY 11724

Travel Notes

Travel Notes